hiS Tis a FOCFBALL CLUB.

THE LITTLE BOOK OF
LIVERPOOL

A LIVERPOOL A to Z

Written by Michael Heatley

THE LITTLE BOOK OF
LIVERPOOL

This edition first published in the UK in 2007
By Green Umbrella Publishing

© Green Umbrella Publishing 2007

www.greenumbrella.co.uk

Publishers Jules Gammond and Vanessa Gardner

Printed and bound in China

ISBN: 978-1-906229-46-7

Contents

ALDRIDGE

Aldridge

caption
RIGHT Aldridge taking his penalty kick in the 1988 FA Cup Final

BELOW Aldridge celebrates scoring against Nottingham Forest, 1989

STRIKER JOHN ALDRIDGE WAS born in Liverpool in 1958, but he was in his thirtieth year before he made his Anfield debut. He started with Newport County, playing his first game in the 1979-80 season, before moving to

Oxford United. Having scored more than 150 goals at his first two clubs, he signed on at Anfield in 1987.

Aldridge may have missed from the penalty spot in the 1988 FA Cup Final against Wimbledon, but he proved to be a prolific goalscorer for his new club in the league, netting 50 goals in 83 games. His career at Anfield was however comparatively short. Having teamed up magnificently with Peter Beardsley, Aldridge left for Real Sociedad after Ian Rush returned from Juventus to eventually reclaim his place in the Liverpool side.

Aldridge did well in Spain, but arguably did even better when he returned to England and signed for Tranmere Rovers in 1991. His career seemed to be drawing to a close, but he continued to score freely at Prenton Park, netting 40 goals in his first season there. Prior to his move to Tranmere, Aldridge had helped Jack Charlton's Republic of Ireland side to a quarter-final place in the 1990 World Cup.

4 | THE LITTLE BOOK OF LIVERPOOL

All-time Attendance Records

FOR COMPARISON'S SAKE, THE capacity of today's all-seater Anfield is 45,362; figures in excess of this were of course established when both ends of the ground were standing terraces.

ABOVE A familiar sight, a passionate Liverpool crowd

HIGHEST LEAGUE ATTENDANCE: 58,757 v Chelsea (1949)

HIGHEST FA CUP ATTENDANCE: 61,905 v Wolves (1952) fifth round

HIGHEST LEAGUE CUP ATTENDANCE: 50,880 v Nottingham Forest (1980) semi-final second leg

HIGHEST EUROPEAN ATTENDANCE: 55,104 v Barcelona (1976) semi-final second leg

LOWEST FA CUP ATTENDANCE (POST-WAR) 11,207 v Chester City, 1945-46 third round second leg

LOWEST LEAGUE ATTENDANCE: 1,000 v Loughborough Town (1895)

LOWEST LEAGUE ATTENDANCE: (POST-WAR) 11,976 v Scunthorpe United (1959) Division 2

LOWEST FA CUP ATTENDANCE: 4,000 v Newton (1892) second Qualifying Round

LOWEST LEAGUE CUP ATTENDANCE: 9,902 v Brentford (1983) second round second leg

LOWEST EUROPEAN ATTENDANCE: 12,021 Dundalk (1982) European Cup first round first leg

All-time Team

1	Ray Clemence
2	Chris Lawler
3	Emlyn Hughes
4	Alan Hansen
5	Ron Yeats
6	Graeme Souness
7	Kevin Keegan
8	Roger Hunt
9	Kenny Dalglish
10	Steven Gerrard
11	Ian Callaghan

Subs

12	Tommy Lawrence
14	Steve Heighway
15	Michael Owen
16	Ian St John
17	Ian Rush

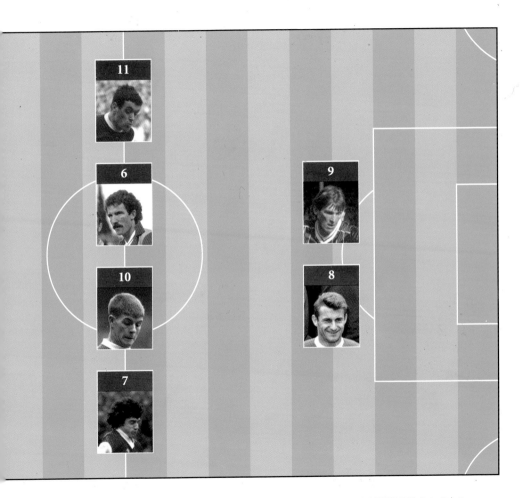

Anfield

ANFIELD IS, IN MANY WAYS, THE key to the continued success of the team that plays there. A sign over the tunnel leading from the dressing rooms to the pitch reminds visitors that 'This Is Anfield' – a warning that's superfluous the moment opposing players feel the grass beneath their boots. Because the vocal support Liverpool's fans have given their team over the years is second to none. Go back to 1884, of course, and it was Everton that originally inhabited the embryonic stadium, moving across to Stanley Park in 1892 - since which time it's been red through and through!

The whole tradition of community singing and terrace chanting started here, each song laced with traditional Scouse humour. And though

RIGHT Liverpool play to a capacity crowd at Anfield

BELOW The famous players tunnel at Anfield

the Anfield Road terrace was given seats in 1983, the opposite behind-goal terrace, the Spion Kop, remained a hotbed of singing, swaying support envied the world over until Anfield finally had to bow to the demands of safety and turn all-seater in 1994. Two years before that, an upper tier had been added to the Kemlyn Road stand, which thereby became the Centenary Stand. A similar second tier was added to the Anfield Road stand in 1998, bringing the capacity up to an impressive 45,362.

Other additions to the ground in recent years to highlight significant people and events have included the

Shankly Gates, erected in 1982 in memory of the legendary manager Bill Shankly who passed away the previous year, the Paisley Gateway, erected outside the Kop in 1999 in honour of the club's most successful manager ever,

and the eternal flame of the Hillsborough Memorial dedicated to the 96 fans who so tragically lost their lives in 1989.

Anfield has been used to host international games, most notably the Scotland versus Wales World Cup qualifier in 1977, and, while Goodison Park was Merseyside's World Cup venue in 1966 when England hosted the final stages, it was Anfield that, 30 years later, hosted four games in Euro '96 (Eire and Holland having already met in a qualifying play-off). But then Anfield had staged its first international, between England and Ireland, as far back as 1889!

In 2002, Liverpool Football Club revealed plans to build a new stadium in Stanley Park – but you can bet there will be many fans who shed more than a tear if and when it ever happens.

ABOVE Anfield viewed from the outside

LEFT Paisley Gateway entrance at Anfield

Barnes

JAMAICAN-BORN JOHN BARNES, the son of a diplomat, came into this world on 7 November 1963. He was a sensational goalscorer with Watford,

BELOW John Barnes
runs with the ball

helping them climb to the top division, before he moved to Anfield for a then-record £900,000 fee in 1987. Already capped by England, his international performances had not gone uncriticised, although he had scored one magnificent goal in Brazil's Maracana Stadium. Altogether, he was to play 79 times in an England shirt, a total that speaks for itself.

Kenny Dalglish was convinced that Barnes would be a considerable

asset to his side, and to begin with he certainly was: he scored 61 goals in his first four seasons, mainly from midfield, and he helped Liverpool to two League championships, the FA Cup and the League Cup. He slowed up a bit as time went on but he could still be effective as a midfield anchor.

Barnes left for Newcastle United in August 1997, but by then his playing career was drawing to its close. Following limited managerial experience at Celtic (he lasted for just 20 games before being sacked) he has now established himself as a competent and very likeable television presenter.

LEFT Barnes in action for Liverpool against Sheffield Wednesday, 1995

BELOW Barnes takes on Robert Lee of Newcastle, 1994

BAROS

Baros

MUCH CRITICISED by Liverpool fans since his arrival from Banik Ostrava in December 2001 for a reported £3.4 mil-

RIGHT Baros scores the winning goal from a penalty, against Crystal Palace, 2004

BELOW Baros controls the ball for Liverpool

lion, the rangy, six-foot Czech international striker (born 28 October 1981) has nevertheless proved his class since making his Reds debut in Barcelona in March 2002. He claimed two goals on his Premiership bow against Bolton, scoring three times in his first six domestic games. But he'd had to wait for a work permit and arrived at the same time as Nicolas Anelka, so it took time for him to establish a similar reputation as at home, where he was known as the 'Ostravan Maradona'.

He was top scorer in Euro 2004, scoring five times as his country reached the semi-finals and this made up for suffering a broken leg early in the domestic season that restricted him to 13 Premiership appearances. But while his role in Rafa Benitez's first Anfield campaign was often and unavoidably that of a lone striker as injuries decimated the Reds' strike force, he joint top-scored with 13. His strike rate for club (27 in 106 games) and country (22 in 36 games) is as healthy as anyone's. He left for Aston Villa in the summer of 2005.

Beardsley

IN TERMS OF STAR QUALITY, Peter Beardsley was a late developer. Born in Newcastle in 1961, he began his professional career with Carlisle United in 1979, but he then wandered between Vancouver Whitecaps and Manchester United (for whom he made no League appearances) until he signed for his home-town club in 1983. There, along with Kevin Keegan and Chris Waddle, his predatory striking skills helped Newcastle gain promotion to the top flight.

The diminutive striker had arrived, and in time he was to play for his country on 59 occasions. Following some exuberant appearances in the 1986 World Cup, Beardsley was signed by Kenny Dalglish in July 1987 for £1.9 million. He soon began knocking in the goals for his new club. Although he scored 46 times in 131 League games, Dalglish often left him out of the side after his first season, and when Graeme Souness took over as manager he sold Beardsley to Everton for £1 million.

Peter Beardsley was wandering once more. After two years at Everton, he went back to Newcastle, where he was welcomed as a returning hero – and scored another 47 League goals. Before he hung up his boots, he played for Bolton Wanderers, Manchester City, Fulham, Hartlepool United, Doncaster Rovers and Melbourne Knights.

ABOVE Beardsley goes past Gary Pallister of Manchester United during the FA Charity Shield of 1990

LEFT Beardsley in action for Liverpool

Benitez

BORN ON 16 APRIL 1960, RAFAEL Benitez's coaching CV began with Real Madrid's youth team at the age of 26 after injury wrecked his career as a player. His first managerial attempt with Valladolid resulted in the sack, but promotions with Extremadura and Tenerife set up a dream job with Valencia in 2001. In his three seasons there he took them to their first title for 31 years and a La Liga/UEFA Cup double in 2003-04 before deciding to test his skills further and move on to the Premiership.

His early days at Anfield saw fans slow to warm to Benitez, his predecessor Gerard Houllier having been extremely popular. The predominance of Spanish players and backroom staff arriving was also noted. But who can now say the choice wasn't inspired? "When I arrived," he said after the Reds' European triumph, "I was thinking about being in the top four and maybe getting to a cup final. I knew that would be difficult but now I'm happy with what we've done."

A comfortable top three finish and FA Cup Final win in 2005-06 in what was a season of transition encouraged Benitez to pledge his future to the Reds, despite interest from Real Madrid.

Boot Room

THE ANFIELD 'BOOT ROOM', where the coaching staff met to plot future games over a cup of tea or, occasionally, something stronger, would become a notable breeding ground for future Liverpool bosses. Bob Paisley, though almost unknown outside the city when he took the job on (some claim against his better judgement), would eclipse even 'Shanks' in terms of trophies won when he succeeded to the throne in 1974. Boot-room regular Joe Fagan would hold the reins briefly from 1983 to 1985, his successful spell soured by Heysel. When Kenny Dalglish, elevated from player to manager, quit in 1989 after Hillsborough, caretaker-manager Ronnie Moran emerged from the boot room to lead the team to a morale-boosting 7-1 win at Derby.

Roy Evans became assistant to incoming manager Graeme Souness, and when things fell apart in

ABOVE Ronnie Moran caretaker-manager for Liverpool in 1991

LEFT An emotional Roy Evans shakes hands with Liverpool chairman David Moores as he leaves the club after 33 years service, signalling the end of the boot room tradition in 1998

BOOT ROOM

RIGHT Phil Thompson and Gerard Houllier show their frustration during an Aston Villa game, 2003

BELOW Sammy Lee displays his diplomacy skills as he intervenes between Jamie Carragher and Sheffield United manager Neil Warnock

early 1994 he was on hand to pick up the pieces. Unfortunately little was achieved during his reign and the arrival of Houllier, initially in a joint managerial capacity, was the beginning of the end. Nevertheless, the unassuming ex-full back had contributed greatly to Liverpool's success over the years.

Another former player and boot-room regular, Phil Thompson, became Houllier's assistant, taking over during

his heart scare. Sammy Lee, a former midfielder, also played a backstage part until lured away to the England staff.

These days under Benitez the boot room speaks with a predominantly foreign accent. Currently employed are assistant manager Pako Ayesteran, first-team coaches Alex Miller and Paco Herrera, reserve-team manager Hughie McAuley, goalkeeping coach Jose Ochotorena, chief scout Ron Yeats and academy director Steve Heighway.

Callaghan

'CALLY', JUST TURNED 18, WAS applauded off the field by his team-mates after his first-team debut for Liverpool – against Bristol Rovers in April 1960 – and went on to rack up applause, awards and medals galore in a marathon career at Anfield.

Born on 10 April 1942, Ian Callaghan was the only Liverpool player to appear for them during their Second Division days and still be there as the European Cup was hoisted in 1977. A direct right-winger in his early days but later used in midfield, Cally comfortably became the holder of the club's appearance record, playing 857 times – almost 200 clear of Emlyn Hughes and Ray Clemence – before moving to Swansea in 1978.

He scored 69 goals for the Reds, 49 of them in the League. Once Liverpool, and Ian Callaghan, won the Second Division championship in 1961-62,

they went from strength to strength, winning five First Division titles, the FA Cup twice, the UEFA Cup twice plus the European Cup and European Super Cup. And on a personal level, Callaghan was the Football Writers' Player of the Year in 1974 and was awarded the MBE.

He played four times for England, twice in the early stages of the 1966 World Cup competition, but curiously had to wait another eleven years before gaining his third cap.

ABOVE Callaghan runs with the ball, 1967
BELOW Ian Callaghan pictured with Bob Paisley after Liverpool's victory in the 1977 European Cup Final

Carragher

SIX-FOOTER 'CARRA' IS SURELY Liverpool's unsung hero. Born on Merseyside on 28 January 1978, he has only ever wanted to play for his home-town team, and his club form had at the time of writing won him 33 caps as England centre-back despite strong competition from the likes of Ferdinand, Terry and Campbell. "He is one of our best central defenders now," Sven Goran Eriksson confirms, while Italian legend Maldini has rated him "an outstanding defender", a compliment he cherishes. Carragher took the step up as England's most capped Under 21 player ever, his full debut coming in April 1999 against Hungary.

Not the most comfortable player on the ball, Carragher's speciality is the game-changing tackle; his

competitive qualities mean he has also played at full-back. Making his club debut in the 1996-97 campaign, he scored a rare goal on his Premiership debut that season at Anfield against

RIGHT Carragher scores in the penalty shoot-out during the Worthington Cup Final match against Birmingham City, 2001

BELOW Carragher looks where to make his next pass

Aston Villa. He was a regular choice in red by 1998-99 and is now on his way to 400 appearances in all competitions. Having missed much of 2003-04 with a broken leg, he fought back and made up for lost time with his most successful campaign yet. Much is expected of the latest local boy to make good.

ABOVE Jamie Carragher heads the ball against Watford, 2005

Case

TOUGH-TACKLING, HARD-WORKing midfielder Jimmy Case (born on 18 May 1954) arrived at Anfield in May 1973 for a bargain £500 from non-League South Liverpool. In the following eight seasons he topped 250 appearances and scored 46 goals, many of them thunderous efforts.

After making his debut on the final day of the 1974-75 season, Case made 39 first team appearances in all in 1975-76. He helped Liverpool to the UEFA Cup that season, weighing in with all three home goals as Slask Wroclaw of Poland were beaten 5-1. His intervention proved crucial in the Final, too. Liverpool, two-down inside 12 minutes of the home leg, sent on Case for John Toshack and he inspired a magnificent comeback, scoring the Reds' second goal in a 3-2

RIGHT Case playing for Liverpool in the Charity Shield, 1979

BELOW Jimmy Case in action during a match against Everton at Anfield in 1977

success. A 1-1 draw in the second leg meant a second UEFA Cup success for Liverpool.

At Wembley in 1977 he scored with a wonderful shot on the turn to equalise against Manchester United in the FA Cup Final. In the next few seasons Case linked well with Graeme Souness, Terry McDermott and Ray Kennedy in the Reds' engine room before being ousted in 1980-81 by Sammy Lee. By this time he had, among others, three European Cup medals and four League championship medals to show for his efforts. Case moved to Brighton, a club he later managed, in the summer of 1981.

Charity/ Community Shield

THE FA CHARITY SHIELD (now Community Shield) is the traditional curtain-raiser to the English domestic football campaign, played between the winners of the Premier League and the FA Cup. The first Charity Shield match played in 1908 between Manchester United and Queens Park Rangers was professionals versus amateurs.

It was moved to coincide with the start of the new season in 1959, and has kept its place in the football calendar ever since. In 1974, FA Secretary Ted Croker proposed it should be played at Wembley as official curtain-raiser to the season, and it was Liverpool who celebrated this upgrade with a 6-5 penalty shootout against Leeds United after a 1-1 draw memorable for the uncharitable behaviour of Billy Bremner and Kevin Keegan, who both made history by being sent off. (Since then, teams finishing level have shared the Shield for

six months apiece before the penalty shoot-out was re-introduced in 1993.)

Liverpool have won the Charity Shield 15 times, in 1964 (shared), 1965 (shared), 1966, 1974, 1976, 1977 (shared), 1979, 1980, 1982, 1986 (shared), 1988, 1989 1990 (shared), 2001 and 2006. Perhaps the most memorable Charity Shield encounter apart from the 1974 game was the one in 1992 when Leeds took their revenge for 1974 in a seven-goal thriller.

ABOVE Graeme Souness, Alan Hansen and Kenny Dalglish hold the Charity Shield after defeating Arsenal in 1979

Crouch

PETER CROUCH (BORN 30 January 1981) stands out on any football pitch with a height of 2.01m / 6ft 7in. He failed to make the grade at Tottenham and arrived at Anfield via QPR, Portsmouth, Aston Villa, Norwich (loan) and Southampton. When Saints were relegated Crouch joined Liverpool for £7 million.

Crouch was subject to intense media attention as he was unable to score for his first 19 games in red. After the goal drought ended in December 2005 he went on to score 12 more times that season, including the only goal in the fifth round of the FA Cup against Manchester United, Liverpool's first postwar victory over them in the Cup.

In May 2005, Crouch made his senior England debut against Colombia and went on to feature in the 2006 World Cup qualifying campaign. He scored his first goal in a friendly against Uruguay, another against Hungary inspiring a headline-making robotic dance in celebration. Crouch became the first player ever to reach ten goals for England within a single calendar year and remained a part of the national set-up under Steve McClaren,

Crouch was a victim of squad rotation in the 2006-07 season, but scored the first hat-trick of his club career against Arsenal in March, with goals scored from his right foot, left foot and head.

Clemence

GIVEN THAT RAY CLEMENCE WAS in time to become one of England's greatest goalkeepers, it is perhaps surprising that he was initially press-ganged into putting on the jersey by his school sports master. Born in Skegness on 5 August 1948, he preferred playing in the outfield, but he took to goalkeeping well enough to be offered trials by Notts County and Scunthorpe United – where he was paid £11 a week, and later attracted the attention of Bill Shankly. He made his League debut for Liverpool in 1970, when Tommy Lawrence was injured.

In terms of honours earned, his Liverpool debut marked the start of one of the most successful careers in modern football. Playing behind one of the best-organised defences in the country, between 1971 and 1981 Clemence helped his side to the League Championship five times, the FA Cup,

LEFT Clemence catches the ball in mid air, 1975

CLEMENCE

the League Cup, the European Cup (three times) and the UEFA Cup (twice). He also earned a runners-up medal in two FA Cup Finals and in the League Cup. He was to play a total of 666 games for Liverpool in all competitions, and in 1978-79 he set a First Division record when he conceded just 16 goals in 42 games.

Clemence was lithe and supple, and able to reach the most difficult of shots. He was one of the first goalkeepers to act as an additional sweeper, by moving outside the penalty area before the opposing forward could get to the ball. Had it not been for the presence of Peter Shilton, he would have played in far more than the 61 internationals he graced over an 11-year period. As it was, he kept 27 clean sheets in those 61 matches, during a period when the England side was not at its best. In all, he played in 12 World Cup qualifying matches but never got near to playing in a World Cup Final. It was a similar story when it came to European Championship matches, although Clemence did feature in two games played in the 1980 finals in Italy.

Before his international career drew to a close, Clemence moved to Tottenham Hotspur. He was 33 years old and the move surprised many. He was far from finished however. He played more than 300 games for Spurs, helping them lift the FA Cup in 1982. Raymond Neal Clemence OBE retired due to injury during the 1987-88 season, having played in a remarkable total of 1,119 matches.

Dalglish

NOBODY WHO HAS HEARD HIM speak will be surprised to learn that Kenny Dalglish comes from Glasgow. Having been born there in 1951, he joined Celtic and made more than 200 appearances for the Bhoys before moving to Anfield in August 1977 as replacement for Kevin Keegan. Bob Paisley knew he had a bargain. "His genius is not only in his own ability but in making others play", he said.

Dour and uncommunicative off the field, Dalglish seemed to have an entirely different personality when he was playing. Though he failed to score on his debut, the goalless Charity Shield clash with Manchester United, he would notch 118 League goals in red, 172 first-team goals in total, as well as making countless more for others. His 1978 European Cup-winning strike against Bruges at Wembley capped a sensational

first season, and he was not to disappoint thereafter. International honours continued, too. In all, he was capped 102 times by Scotland, 54 of these coming while at Anfield.

During June 1985, before the end of an outstanding career as a Liverpool

ABOVE Dalglish runs with the ball during the Milk Cup Final against Manchester United in 1983

player (during which time he featured in 355 League games and picked up enough medals to fill a couple of bedside cabinets) Dalglish took over as player-manager. If anyone worried about his mastery of the transfer market, the acquisition of the likes of John Barnes, Peter Beardsley and Jamie Redknapp proved otherwise. And John Aldridge was bought to replace Ian Rush just as Dalglish had replaced Keegan.

Liverpool won the Double the following season, and went on to win two more League titles while Dalglish was at the helm, fellow Scot Alan Hansen his captain and voice on the pitch. It was therefore to the dismay of many Reds fans that 'King Kenny' quit the manager's job in 1991, claiming the stress factor was too great. His sudden departure mirrored that of fellow Scot and legend Bill Shankly, but the strain of Hillsborough and its aftermath (in which he played an unsung part consol-

ing the bereaved) was clearly a contributory factor.

An enigmatic character, Dalglish was soon managing again, this time at Blackburn Rovers where he successfully teamed up with the late Ray Harford (although it's hard to know quite how they managed to understand each other's accents) and later at Newcastle United. He is currently out of the game, but could walk into almost any job he wished on the strength of past achievements.

Derby Matches

LOCAL DERBIES ARE, BY DEFINI-
tion, hard-fought affairs. Whether
you're in Manchester, Glasgow, London
or Liverpool, no quarter will be given
and no prisoners taken. Yet few derby
matches are played in the same uniquely
humorous spirit as the Merseyside clash
between Liverpool and Everton. The
city's penchant for ready wit is well
chronicled, having turned out a wealth

of professional funnymen from Jimmy
Tarbuck to Alexei Sayle. But on derby
day, every one of the supporters packed
into Goodison Park or Anfield is ready
and willing to add their own page to the
history of the fixture.

The first League derby between the
teams took place at Goodison Park on
13 October 1894, and it was the Blues
who drew first blood in a 3-0 win. The
return saw honours even at 2-2, but
Liverpool found the First Division
somewhat inhospitable and subsided

ABOVE Steven Gerrard
is shown the red card
after his foul on
Everton's Kevin
Campbell (on the
ground) in 1999

DERBY MATCHES

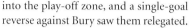

RIGHT Thomas
Graveson of Everton
battles for the ball with
Hamann, 2004

BELOW Adrian Heath
of Everton jumps to
head the ball as Alan
Hansen looks on, 1984

RIGHT Thomas
Graveson of Everton
battles for the ball with
Hamann, 2004

into the play-off zone, and a single-goal reverse against Bury saw them relegated.

A 106-goal record haul took the reds back up with some ease in 1896, putting the Merseyside derby back on the agenda. And that, give or take the odd season, is exactly where it's been for Liverpool and Everton supporters for the century and more that's followed.

The 1980s onwards has seen many different nationalities become involved in Merseyside affairs, with the likes of Preki (Yugoslavia), Warzycha (Poland) and Kearton (Australia) doing battle with the likes of Kozma (Hungary), Piechnik (Denmark) and Bjornebye (Norway). Most interesting of all though was Jan Molby, a Dane who became an adopted Scouser. It should be remembered, though, that the very first team Liverpool fielded in 1892 contained not one Merseysider... in fact, all eleven members of the 'team of the macs' were Scots! So Liverpool v Everton derbies have always had their cosmopolitan side. The 1980s also brought two FA Cup Final meetings, both of which are profiled in detail elsewhere.

In the long history of Merseyside derbies, which game has been the greatest of all time? In living memory, many people's money will be on the FA Cup Fifth Round replay of 1991. The 4-4 draw had a sensational sting in the tail when Anfield legend Kenny Dalglish revealed it was his last match in charge. Ironically, it would be the man who succeeded him, Graeme Souness, who ran into heart problems, because this pulsating 120 minutes had absolutely everything. Suffice to say that four Liverpool goals found four Everton ripostes, confirming, as if confirmation were needed, that the Merseyside derby remained one of football's most passionately contested fixtures.

Dudek

SIGNED FROM DUTCH CLUB Feyenoord in the summer of 2001 for £5.5 million to replace error-prone Sander Westerveld, Polish international Jerzy Dudek (born on 23 March 1973) had played 136 games for the Dutch side after joining from Sokol Tychy and established himself as first choice for his country. He had the misfortune, however, to join Liverpool in a relatively fallow period, and also to make a few televised howlers. Despite figuring for Poland in the 2002 World Cup, the League Cup in 2003 was his only honour in the red (or should that be green) of Liverpool until the 2005 Champions League Final gave him the platform to put on a match-winning performance in what was billed as his final game for the Reds.

His rubber-legged goal-line theatrics, inspired by Bruce Grobbelaar, had the desired effect and his saves from Shevchenko – a penalty, preceded by a stunning double stop from the same player in open play – secured the silverware. Dudek saw off challenges to his place from promising England hopefuls Chris Kirkland and Scott Carson, but the arrival of Pepe Reina from Villareal in the summer of 2005 appeared to have limited his future chances.

BELOW Jerzy Dudek faces Pirlo of AC Milan in the penalty shoot-out, Champions League Final 2005

BOTTOM Dudek then saves the decisive penalty from AC Milan forward Shevchenko

European Cup

EUROPEAN CUP

ABOVE RIGHT Phil Thompson lifts the European Cup, 1981

RIGHT Liverpool celebrate victory over Bruges in 1978

BELOW A European lap of honour after beating Borussia Moenchengladbach, 1977

LIVERPOOL'S FIRST VENTURE INTO Europe came in the European Cup of 1964-65 after winning their first League title under Shankly. In this competition they were defeated by Inter Milan in the San Siro by 3-0, having won the first leg 3-1. So near yet so far!

Liverpool's record was a model of consistency, qualifying for Europe for 21 consecutive seasons (1964-65 to 1984-85) until the post-Heysel ban. It was a Liverpool trademark that the first team was backed up by an able squad of reserves ready to step in at a moment's notice, and it was this strength in depth that helped them obtain such consistent success.

Liverpool's victory in 2005 was their fifth European Cup (Champions League) success. The first came in 1977, when Bob Paisley's team beat Borussia Moenchengladbach in Rome. Paisley's team talk consisted of the story of him rolling into Rome on the back of a tank

as part of the liberating forces – and thanks to goals from Terry McDermott, Tommy Smith (a rare strike from the veteran defender) and a Phil Neal penalty they liberated the silverware from, er, German hands!

The following season saw them retain their trophy, a single-goal win against Bruges at Wembley functional rather than entertaining. With Kevin Keegan now out of the picture at Hamburg, the Kopites found a new hero in Celtic's Kenny Dalglish. He chipped an unforgettable winner from a Souness through ball to take the title.

Three years then passed until they travelled to Paris to face the mighty Real Madrid, the team with the best European Cup pedigree of them all. Stalemate ruled until, with six minutes left on the clock the Kennedys, Ray and Alan, combined. Surprisingly it was striker turned midfielder Ray

whose quick throw-in sent Alan away to net, but who cared when the result was a Cup hat-trick?

The last European Cup win Liverpool were to register for 21 years came in 1984, against Roma on penalties. Since then there's been the unforgettable comeback from 3-0 down to secure another penalty win in 2005 against AC Milan in Istanbul, and the 2007 Final against the same opposition.

TOP Liverpool celebrate winning the 1984 European Cup Final against AS Roma

BOTTOM Steven Gerrard proudly lifts the Champions League trophy in 2005

FA Cup

BELOW Liverpool in the FA Cup Final of 1914 against Burnley played at Crystal Palace

LIVERPOOL HAD TO WAIT UNTIL 1914 to contest their first Cup Final, and were unfortunate to lose by a single goal to fellow Lancashire outfit Burnley.

The FA Cup would prove an unlucky competition for the Reds, and it wasn't until 1950 that they'd reach the Final again. By now it was at Wembley, and they journeyed south to meet and be beaten by capital club Arsenal. Future boss Bob Paisley had scored on the run-in but was dropped for the Final itself, a rare moment of disappointment for a very successful character.

But defeat at Wembley in 1950 preceded relegation four years later, and the

first win would not occur until well into the Shankly reign. But the victory in 1965 against bitter rivals Leeds was well worth waiting for. Full-back Gerry Byrne played on despite breaking his collarbone in the tenth minute, even managing to set up Roger Hunt who scored the winner in extra-time to make it 2-1!

Wins against Newcastle in 1974, Everton in 1986 and 1989, Sunderland in 1992 and Arsenal in 2001 – the very first time this was played at Cardiff's Millennium Stadium – complete the Reds' FA Cup story to date. In 2006 Liverpool beat West Ham on penalties in one of the most exciting finals for many years, Steve Gerrard scored on two occasions and turned the match around.

ABOVE Led by Alan Hansen, Liverpool celebrate FA Cup victory in 1986

TOP LEFT Liverpool win the FA Cup in 2006, with Steve Gerrard very much hero of the day!

LEFT Captain of Liverpool, Ron Yeats holds the Cup as he is chaired by fellow members of the victorious team, 1965

Famous Fans

MANY FANS TAKE THEIR love of LFC to extremes, and late, great DJ John Peel was no exception. Naming his children William Anfield, Alexandra Anfield, Thomas Dalglish and Florence Shankly betrayed John's continuing love of the club, even though he lived his later years not on Merseyside but in deepest East Anglia. He would often visit Portman Road, home of local team Ipswich Town, but at heart he remained a red.

RIGHT The late great John Peel, DJ

BELOW Comedian Jimmy Tarbuck

Called upon to be a presenter on TV pop television show Top Of The Pops, John would leave the viewer with little doubt as to who he supported; a female relative of the family knitted him a red jumper that simply stated 'League Champions' and then underneath listed each and every year the club had lifted the honour. A year later and John would have a new jumper, newly knitted and bearing testament to the latest success of the men from Anfield. It was a simple yet highly effective statement.

Peel's fellow famous fans range from comedians Stan Boardman and Jimmy Tarbuck to pop stars Ian McCulloch (Echo and the Bunnymen) and Ian Broudie (Lightning Seeds). Cilla Black, Craig Charles of Red Dwarf and DJ Spoony are also numbered among that elite band of celebrity Kopites. Eat your heart out, Delia!

Fagan

BORN ON 12 MARCH 1921, JOE Fagan became Liverpool manager at the ripe old age of 63 after Bob Paisley's retirement and, like his predecessor, had no previous managerial experience. He had, however, been a boot-room fixture since Bill Shankly's arrival and knew the club's workings inside-out.

The first of his two seasons in charge 1983-1984 saw Liverpool win their fourth successive League Cup and third successive League Championship.

Not only that, they brought up a historic treble by winning the European Cup for the fourth time in eight seasons. Few changes were made to Bob Paisley's squad but the breakthrough of striker Ian Rush, signed from Chester in 1980 and a regular in the reserves, was important to the success. Fagan also brought influential Danish midfielder Jan Molby from Ajax.

Fagan's second and final season saw Everton – of all people – take the title with four matches to spare. And, while the Reds reached the European Cup final once again, their intention of retaining their trophy against Italian champions Juventus was rendered meaningless by off-field events at Brussels' Heysel Stadium. It was a sad end to two eventful years.

Fagan was succeeded by striker Kenny Dalglish, who accepted the role of player-manager. He died at the age of 80 in July 2001.

LEFT Joe Fagan (left) pictured in the dug-out at the 1984 European Cup Final

Finnan

REPUBLIC OF IRELAND international, Steve Finnan (born on 24 April 1976) arrived at Anfield for £3.5m from Fulham ahead of the 2003-04 campaign. The attacking right back, prominent as Liverpool charged to Champions League glory in 2005, had far more humble beginnings, starting out at non-league Welling before moving to Birmingham and Notts County.

But it was at Fulham, much closer to his Merton family roots, that he made his mark, being voted the club's player of the year in 2002. That year he figured in Mick McCarthy's World Cup squad. Injury affected his first season at Anfield but Finnan made a big impression in 2004-05, making the starting line-up

RIGHT Steve Finnan and Jlloyd Samuel of Aston Villa go for the same ball, 2004

BELOW Finnan charges with the ball for Liverpool

52 times and even getting on the score sheet in Liverpool's 3-0 win over West Bromwich Albion.

Composed and with a superb first touch, his forays down the right flank have become a feature of many a Liverpool attack and the club's assault on Europe. He inadvertently played a key role in Liverpool's glorious Champions League success – having been the pick of Liverpool's defenders during that torrid first half against AC Milan, a thigh strain prevented him returning to the pitch and the ensuing formation reshuffle assisted the Reds' rousing comeback.

Fowler

ROBBIE FOWLER (born 9 April 1975) grew up an Everton fan and, like his mentor Ian Rush, made the transition from Goodison to Anfield playing staff.

At the age of 18, Fowler impressed during a summer tournament for the England Under-19s and was expected to start the 1993-94 season as a regular for his club. But though he scored all five in a 5-0 drubbing of Fulham and finished the season with 18 he'd wait till the following campaign to link with his idol regularly. The youngster opened his account with a hat-trick against Arsenal and was the club's top scorer, earning a Coca-Cola Cup winner's medal after a 2-1 win over Bolton.

In 1995-96 Fowler made way for Stan Collymore, but came back to score a staggering 36 goals, second only to Alan Shearer, and made a long-awaited debut for England in Euro '96, coming on as substitute four times.

During 1996-97, his understanding with Collymore failed to click, prompting the latter's departure, but scored 31 goals in the season. Then injury struck and, with new boss Gerard Houllier preferring Owen and Heskey up front, Robbie joined Leeds United in a £11million deal in November 2001. An injury-hit stay ended when he moved to Kevin Keegan's Manchester City in January 2003, where he remained until a shock return to Anfield in January 2006. He scored four times in his first 12 games, including a goal on his 31st birthday, as he played for his future.

LEFT Robbie Fowler celebrates after scoring the fourth goal for Liverpool during the UEFA Cup Final, 2001

BELOW Fowler scores for Liverpool against Portsmouth, 2006

Garcia

RIGHT Garcia celebrates his goal against Chelsea, 2005
BELOW Luis Garcia takes a breather during a game

BORN ON 24 JUNE 1978, Barcelona-born Garcia can operate as a winger on either side or a striker, this versatility making him a valuable member of the current Liverpool squad. He proved that value by playing 44 games in his first season and finishing the Reds' joint top scorer with 13 goals.

He signed from his home-town team for £6 million in 2004, but has spent the majority of his playing career on loan to clubs like Valladolid, Tenerife (where 16 goals were scored in 40 games under Rafael Benitez), Toledo and Atletico Madrid. Having played a part in Barcelona's 2003-04 UEFA Cup campaign, he was able to bring this experience to bear for his new club in 2004-05.

Garcia had registered no major honours in his career before coming to Anfield, but this has already changed. He notched three goals in his first seven games for Spain but was suspended for the 2006 FA Cup Final. A truly exciting if sometimes frustrating player who seemingly prefers breathtaking strikes to easy chances, he is a legend in the making.

Gerrard

ALONG WITH CHELSEA'S FRANK Lampard, Whiston-born Steven Gerrard (born on 30 May 1980) is undoubtedly the most influential midfielder in English (and some would say international) football. He made his debut in a red shirt in November 1998 as a substitute against Blackburn, and five years later had been appointed captain by Gerard Houllier. Rafa Benitez was equally sure of Gerrard's value to the team, and struggled to keep him after Chelsea's interest was strongly rumoured in 2004. The following year's European success increased the chance that Gerrard would not 'do a Rooney' and leave the club he'd loved since childhood.

The PFA Young Player of the Year for 1998 has matured swiftly, overcoming persistent growing pains and resulting injury-proneness to make himself indispensable to the cause. His full Liverpool debut came in a UEFA Cup game against Celta Vigo, Kevin Keegan gave him his England bow in May 2000 against the Ukraine and he scored his first goal for his country in September 2001's memorable 5-1 win against Germany. A Liverpool strike in that same season against Manchester United was voted the best Premiership goal ever scored for the club.

It was no coincidence that Liverpool's first goal in the Champions League Final

LEFT Steven Gerrard pictured in 1999

BELOW Gerrard runs with the ball

was a Gerrard header; he's specialised in leading on the front and turning around lost causes. This was a header, but it's powerful strikes from the edge of the area that make him such a threat. He ended the 2005 Champions League final at right-back, hauled into the back line to negate substitute Serginho's threat, but Gerrard would and does play anywhere for the cause and succeeds brilliantly. A total footballer for the 2000s.

"Steve covers lots of ground, goes forward more often and has an impressive shot," says Xabi Alonso of his midfield colleague. Certainly, he can play every midfield role but it is when he is allowed to rampage forward, leaving the sweeping up to others, that he has his biggest effect on games.

As far as his England career goes, he missed the 2002 World Cup through injury but captained his country for the first time against Sweden in 2004, suggesting Gerrard may be the natural successor to David Beckham when the Real Madrid star retires from international football.

Gerrard scored an amazing double for Liverpool to turn around the FA Cup Final against West Ham in 2006 and is still a key man for club and country whether playing wide or in midfield.

LEFT Grobbelaar directs his defence

BELOW Bruce walks on his hands during a match

Grobbelaar

THE SHOCK TRANSFER OF RAY Clemence to Spurs at the start of 1981-82 saw a real goalkeeping character hit Anfield – 24 year-old Bruce Grobbelaar, who soon made a name for himself with his clowning antics and spectacular style.

Grobbelaar was born on 6 October 1957 in South Africa. His family later moved to Rhodesia, and the flamboyant youngster soon developed into an all-round sportsman, representing his adopted country at both cricket and baseball at junior level. Football was his first love, however, and he decided to follow in his father's footsteps and become a goalkeeper.

Problems with work permits meant that he did not begin his league career in England until he signed for Crewe Alexandra, on loan from Vancouver Whitecaps, in 1979. He then returned to Vancouver and finally signed for Liverpool, for £250,000, in March 1981.

Bruce Grobbelaar never believed in standing around and waiting for shots to come his way. He enjoyed dashing to

GROBBELAAR

the edge of his area to catch the ball and surprise advancing forwards, and he managed to surprise quite a few of his own defenders

in the process. His goalkeeping was always spectacular and sometimes suicidal, and he often indulged in bizarre antics during the course of a game. He would run the ball up his back and over his head before clearing, walk on his hands, and engage members of the crowd in conversation. This did not always go down well.

Grobbelaar would doubtless have been forgiven his antics in the early years, had it not been for a number of crucial goalkeeping errors. His habit of charging upfield, his propensity to head the ball out and his dropping of crosses all caused concern. And yet he was clearly an amazingly talented keeper, and he was to play a major part in some remarkably successful Liverpool seasons.

In 1983-84 the Reds won the unique treble of League Championship, League Cup and European Cup. In the Final of the latter competition they faced Roma and, with the game tied at one apiece, the destination of the trophy was to be decided on penalties. Grobbelaar's wobbly legs routine may well have made all the difference: Liverpool won 4-2.

After the Heysel disaster, Bruce Grobbelaar considered giving up football. He changed his mind, however, and helped his side to yet more League and Cup success. He remained at Anfield until a move to Southampton in 1994, by which time the Liverpool faithful had well and truly taken him to their hearts.

The later part of Bruce Grobbelaar's career was dogged by controversy. He was accused of match-fixing while playing for Liverpool but, after five court hearings of various kinds, was eventually exonerated.

Hamann

BORN ON 27 AUGUST 1973, 'Didi' Hamann's retention on a one-year deal for 2005-06 underlined his importance to Liverpool under Rafa Benitez. Introduced at half time in the Champions League Final, the tall German brought all his experience to bear, locking up Milan playmaker Kaka and allowing Steve Gerrard to bomb forward with immediate effect. He is also a noted dead-ball specialist.

Hamann got his first experience of English football with Newcastle and it took a then record £9 million to prize him away from St James' Park in 1999. He was a regular for Germany in the 1998 and 2002 World Cups, as well as the Euro 2000 and 2004 tournaments, and his holding role is a vital one for country as well as club. He scored the final goal at the old (pre-rebuilt) Wembley as Germany beat England in October 2000, the result precipitating former Red Kevin Keegan's departure as national manager.

Hamann boasts the most silverware of any recent Liverpool player, with two UEFA Cup winners medals, German League and Cup, English League Cup and FA Cup, not to mention a World Cup Final appearance – the only Liverpool player bar Roger Hunt to make one – and of course the 2005 Champions League medal richly earned in 75 minutes. Having extended his Anfield tenure by a season, Hamann departed for Bolton Wanderers in summer 2006, but moved on to Manchester City without playing a first-team game.

BELOW Hamann escapes with the ball

BOTTOM Hamann scores for Liverpool against Bayer Leverkusen, 2005

Hansen

A TALL AND SOMEWHAT SKINNY defender called Alan Hansen (born on 13 June 1955) came to Anfield from Partick Thistle in 1977. The 22 year-old had cost just £100,000 and, once he had put on a bit of weight, he proved to be the bargain of a lifetime.

It was a while before Hansen became a first-team regular but, from 1981, he teamed up with Mark Lawrenson to form the solid heart of an excellent Liverpool defence. Hansen was a cultured player and, unlike many centre-halves, always looked comfortable on the ball. He made over 600 appearances for Liverpool, and 26 for Scotland, before injury forced his slightly premature retirement in 1990. Then, although he seemed to be an ideal candidate for management, he decided his destiny lay elsewhere.

Alan Hansen became a television pundit, and he is a very entertaining one. Defensive errors frequently incur his displeasure and, on a Saturday night, many a Premiership footballer must curl up on the sofa with embarrassment as Hansen gets going. He does offer praise from time to time, but he always tries to keep it to a minimum. Hansen was a great player and, as a commentator upon the game, it has to be said he's awesome.

OPPOSITE RIGHT
Alan Hansen celebrates along with the rest of Liverpool after they beat Chelsea at Stamford Bridge to secure the League Championship, 1986

RIGHT Hansen jumps higher for the ball than his Nottingham Forest opponent

Heighway

ONE OF THE COMPARATIVELY FEW professional footballers to have a university degree, Steve Heighway was signed by Liverpool from Skelmersdale United in 1970. Plans to become a teacher were abandoned as Heighway, who was born in Dublin on 25 January 1947 and later attended Warwick University, went on to establish himself as one of Liverpool's finest wingers.

Bob Paisley said he was one of the best amateur players he had ever seen. A fixture in the Liverpool side for most of the 1970s, Heighway had great speed as well as an accurate delivery; striker John Toshack frequently benefiting from his pin-point crosses. He was also a scorer of some tremendous goals, including his side's only strike in the 1971 FA Cup Final against Arsenal. Liverpool lost out on that occasion, but Heighway was soon to collect a chest-full of medals with the Reds.

Between 1970 and 1981, Steve Heighway scored 50 goals in 329 League appearances for Liverpool, but of course he was responsible for many more. During this period he also won 34 caps with the Republic of Ireland team. His playing career almost over, he went to the USA for a while, before returning to Anfield to coach the youth side, he retired in 2007.

Houghton

GLASWEGIAN MIDFIELDER RAY Houghton was born on 9 January 1962. Fulham manager Malcolm Macdonald rescued him from the obscurity of West Ham's reserve side and took him to Craven Cottage in 1982. He did well there, becoming a firm favourite with the Fulham fans before Oxford United – at that time in the top division – paid £150,000 to secure his services. A couple of years later, Kenny Dalglish paid more than five times that sum to take him to Anfield.

Houghton was a hard-working and skilful player, well practised in the ancient art of dribbling. He spent five years at Liverpool, making around 200 appearances in all and scoring 28 League goals. He was then largely replaced in the side by Steve McManaman and was transferred to Aston Villa before later playing for Crystal Palace, and becoming player-coach at Reading.

Having elected to play for the Republic of Ireland, his father's birthplace, rather than Scotland, Houghton soon established himself as a stalwart of the side. He went on to win a total of 73 caps, mainly while Jack Charlton was in charge, and in 1987, no doubt to the delight of his father and the dismay of his mother, he helped the Republic beat Scotland in a European Championship qualifying game. He is now a radio pundit.

BELOW Ray Houghton chases Anton Rogan (left) of Sunderland as Gary Bennett (right) moves in during the FA Cup Final at Wembley, 1992

Houllier

APPOINTED AS JOINT MANAGER – Liverpool's first of that ilk – in July 1998, supplementing existing boss Roy Evans, Gerard Houiller assumed total control four moths later. Born on 3 October 1947, he had begun in management at the age of 26 as player-coach at Le Touquet, which was followed by

BELOW A concerned looking Houllier, contemplating his next move

spells at Noeux Les Mines, Lens and Paris St Germain. He was assistant manager of the French national side between 1988 and 1992 before becoming national coach. An association with

Merseyside had begun with a spell as a trainee teacher decades before his second coming.

Houllier's time at Anfield as manager was attended with success, an incredible six-month period from early 2001 seeing the Worthington, FA UEFA, Community Shield and European Super Cup added to the club's trophy haul. But the game against Anfield in October 2001 saw him taken ill with heart problems, and he was rushed to hospital. He resumed the reins from assistant Phil Thompson in March 2002.

He was given two more seasons to add to the 2003 League Cup that was Liverpool's only other honour gained after his extraordinary opening spell, but too many signings like Diouf, Diao and Cheyrou proved ineffective and he was replaced by Rafa Benitez in 2004.

The name of Gerard Houllier, however, remains respected at Anfield as it is throughout football, and he was invited to be a part of the Champions League Final party in respect for his achievements. In summer 2005 he was appointed coach of French champions Olympic Lyon, and helped his new club retain its title with four games still to play.

Hughes

WHETHER IT WAS AS SKIPPER OF Liverpool or, later as one of TV's Question of Sport captains, you knew what you'd get from Emlyn Hughes: boundless energy and maximum, infectious effort. Born on 28 August 1947, he was a natural on the big stage, playing 62 times for England, with 23 of those as captain, and was ultimately awarded an OBE for services to the sport.

LEFT Crazy Horse enters the pitch, 1975
BELOW Hughes pictured playing for Liverpool in 1970

Signed from Blackpool by Bill Shankly for £65,000 aged only 19, Hughes was nothing if not versatile: he made his Liverpool debut as a left-back in 1967 but played anywhere at the back or in midfield, where he had much more freedom to attack. He netted his first Reds goal in August 1967 in a 6-0 trouncing of Newcastle, but another key detail from that game was a rugged tackle which, along

HUGHES

RIGHT Emlyn Hughes
lifts the European Cup
in 1977

with his trademark surging runs, earned him the nickname of Crazy Horse.

In 1977 Hughes became the first Liverpool captain to lift the European Cup, as Borussia Moenchengladbach were beaten 3-1, and he repeated the feat a year later as Liverpool overcame Bruges 1-0. In all he won five League Championships at Anfield, plus a pair of UEFA Cup winners' medals and an FA Cup winners medal and, on a personal level, was named the Football Writers' Player of the Year in 1977. After 12 magical seasons at Anfield Hughes moved to Wolves, leading them to the League Cup in 1980. He died in 2004.

Hunt

ROGER HUNT WAS ONE OF England's heroes in the 1966 World Cup. Born on 20 July 1938 in Golborne, near Warrington, he played initially for Stockton Heath before signing on at Anfield in May 1959. At the time, Liverpool were experiencing life in the relative obscurity of the old Second Division, and were struggling to regain top-flight status. Phil Taylor brought the aspiring inside-forward to Merseyside, but it was under the inspirational managership of Bill Shankly that Hunt, although never particularly speedy, became one of the best forwards in the country. He was awarded his first England cap during the 1961-62 season, even though he was still not playing at the top.

Hunt scored 21 goals in the 1959-60 season, but his side narrowly failed to win promotion, finishing third behind Aston Villa and Cardiff City. Liverpool came third again in the following year's campaign, but in 1961-62 the Reds finally topped the table. They scored 99 goals in their 42 matches, and Hunt netted 41 of them.

With 'Sir' Roger Hunt (as the Kop dubbed him) knocking in the goals, Liverpool were League champions in 1964 and 1966, FA Cup winners in 1965, European Cup semi-finalists, also in 1965, and European Cup Winners Cup runners-up in 1966. Meanwhile, Hunt's England career blossomed, culminating in his World Cup Final appearance at

BELOW Roger Hunt (second from bottom left) pictured with the Cup winning 1965 Liverpool team

HUNT

Park club, before calling it a day. By the time he retired in 1973, the modest Roger Hunt, who claimed that he would have scored far fewer goals had he not played alongside some of the best players in the land, had featured in 34 full international matches, scoring 18 goals. Given his international scoring rate was more than a goal every two games, he probably deserved to have played in more.

Unlike many ex-players, Roger Hunt had no desire to remain in the game when his playing days were over, preferring instead to work in his family's haulage business.

the expense of Jimmy Greaves. However, no-one could say he didn't deserve it, as he had scored three times in the earlier group games. And even though he didn't score in the Final, his contribution to that memorable occasion was also very significant.

Having scored a remarkable total of 245 goals in 404 League matches, Roger Hunt was rather surprisingly transferred by Bill Shankly to Second Division Bolton Wanderers in 1969. Now 31, he was a little less prolific, but he still managed to score 24 times in 76 League appearances for the Burnden

Hyypia

ARRIVING AT ANFIELD in 1999 from Dutch side Willem II, centre-back Hyypia (born 7 October 1973) was an instant success, and outlasted more famous fellow Finn Jari Litmanen to play a role in six seasons of Liverpool football. He led the team when they won five trophies in 2001 (European Super Cup, Community Shield, UEFA Cup and the two domestic cups), but his role since has been less certain. Steve Gerrard has taken on the skipper's mantle, but Hyypia has nevertheless seen off several centre-back partners. He played every Champions League game, while his goal against Juventus in the quarter-final first leg did much to keep Liverpool on track for Champions League glory.

While a six-footer who is dominant in the air, Hyypia (who began his career in Finland with MYPA-47 before moving to Holland in 1995) is very confident on the ground for such a big man. He is also temperamentally sound, having got through they 2000-01 campaign without incurring a single yellow card. With the arrival and departure of Pellegrino in 2004-05, this seasoned campaigner and likeable character was able to continue his partnership with Jamie Carragher, and is contracted to the Reds until 2008.

LEFT Hyypia controls the ball for Liverpool

BELOW Sami Hyypia scores the equalising goal during a match against Spurs, 2005

Internationals

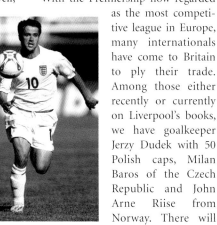

LIVERPOOL FOOTBALL CLUB HAS provided a host of international players down the years – enough to fill a whole book. The first was Harry Bradshaw, who played for England in a 6-0 drubbing of Ireland in 1897. Many more followed, including Rab Howell, also in the late 1890s, who is thought to be the only true Romany to have donned an England shirt.

Since then, an awful lot of famous names have worn the shirts of the home countries, including Roger Hunt, Ray Clemence, Emlyn Hughes, Kevin Keegan, Peter Beardsley, Michael Owen, David James, Emile Heskey and

Liverpool captain Steven Gerrard for England, Billy Liddell, Ian St John and Kenny Dalglish (102 in all) for Scotland, John Toshack for Wales and Ray Houghton for the Republic. Of course, there have been many, many more.

With the Premiership now regarded as the most competitive league in Europe, many internationals have come to Britain to ply their trade. Among those either recently or currently on Liverpool's books, we have goalkeeper Jerzy Dudek with 50 Polish caps, Milan Baros of the Czech Republic and John Arne Riise from Norway. There will no doubt be a great many more in the future.

Liverpool's teams originally drew from the 'Home Countries' (England, Scotland, Wales and Northern Ireland) plus Eire. We reproduce the top five players to have represented these 'traditional' countries while with Liverpool, with the exception of Northern Ireland which has, for some reason, been poorly represented.

ENGLAND TOP FIVE

Caps	Player
66	Michael Owen
59	Emlyn Hughes
56	Ray Clemence
50	Phil Neal
48	John Barnes

SCOTLAND TOP FIVE

Caps	Players
55	Kenny Dalglish
37	Graeme Souness
28	Billy Liddell
27	Steve Nicol
26	Alan Hansen

WALES TOP FIVE

Caps	Player
67	Ian Rush
26	John Toshack
18	Joey Jones
16	Maurice Parry
10	Ernest Peake

NORTHERN IRELAND TOP THREE

Caps	Player
27	Elisha Scott
12	Billy Lacey
03	David Mullen

REPUBLIC OF IRELAND TOP FIVE

Caps	Player
51	Ronnie Whelan
38	Steve Staunton
34	Ray Houghton
33	Steve Heighway
25	Phil Babb

ABOVE Elisha Scott in his playing days for Northern Ireland

LEFT Scotland's Kenny Dalglish in action

Johnston

RIGHT Craig Johnston scores for Liverpool in the 1986 FA Cup Final

BELOW Johnston jumps for the ball in the 1988 FA Cup Final against Wimbledon

CRAIG JOHNSTON WAS an enthusiastic, if unconventional footballer. Born in Johannesburg on 8 December 1960, but brought up in Australia, he joined Liverpool from Middlesborough for a £650,000 fee in 1981. He seemed to get on all right with Bob Paisley, the manager who signed him, but he was something of a rebel and there was to be frequent conflict with Joe Fagan when the latter took over from Paisley.

Midfielder Johnston, nicknamed 'The Headless Chicken' by Paisley, had a tremendous amount of energy, and it seemed he did not burn it all up on the football field. There were frequent rows and arguments and in 1984, having been taken off during the League Cup Final, he walked out before being presented to the Queen. Whether or not Her Majesty was amused, or whether indeed she noticed, is not recorded.

Johnston suffered from a loss of confidence during his time at Anfield, but this returned when Kenny Dalglish took over as manager. Nevertheless, the headless chicken decided to cluck off at the age of 27, having made 190 League appearances for Liverpool, with 30 goals to his credit. He returned to Australia to care for his invalid sister and develop the Predator football boot.

Kay

BORN IN 1891, GEORGE KAY WAS West Ham's captain in the famous White Horse Cup Final of 1923 and had previously been the first Englishman to captain an Irish League club while at Belfast Celtic. Just as his playing career was affected by the First World War George Kay's managerial prowess was interrupted by its successor.

After a five-year stint with Southampton, Kay became Liverpool boss in 1936; his first job was to steer the Reds away from the relegation places. He not only succeeded but went on to be an outstanding manager, one of his pre-war signings being a certain 17 year-old Billy Liddell. Later signings included Bob Paisley, from Bishop Auckland, and Albert Stubbins – the latter from under the noses of Everton. When foot-

ball resumed after the hostilities the deep-thinking Kay masterminded a Reds tour of the USA that helped to foster team spirit.

A fit and confident Liverpool started the 1946-47 season in style and went on to take the League championship. Kay also guided Liverpool to the 1950 FA Cup Final, won by Arsenal 2-0, but by then he was struggling with his health and in January 1951 he stood down on doctors' orders. He died a premature death in 1965; after which the great Billy Liddell said: "If any man gave his life for a club, George Kay did so for Liverpool".

BELOW George Kay (far right) pictured with the 1949 Liverpool team

Keegan

JOSEPH KEVIN KEEGAN WAS BORN on 14 February 1951 in Armthorpe, near Doncaster. Originally simply a promising young midfielder, he scored 18 goals in 124 League appearances for Scunthorpe United, before being signed by Bill Shankly for a paltry £35,000 in May 1971.

Shankly converted his new signing into an all-out striker, and for the next few seasons Keegan and John Toshack formed a formidable duo. Keegan turned out to be one of the most exciting players ever to grace the Anfield arena and it was not long before he achieved pop-star status, even though his actual pop song 'Head Over Heels in Love' barely scraped into the Top 40 in 1979.

Kevin Keegan made his England debut in 1972, and went on to play for his country on another 62 occasions, scoring 21 goals. For several years, he was a key member of the side. On the home front, he scored more than 200 goals in a Liverpool shirt before, to everyone's surprise, he opted to move to SV Hamburg for a half-million-pound

BELOW Keegan goes in for a tackle

fee in 1977. Liverpool's loss was Hamburg's gain, as Keegan went on to be voted European Player of the Year on two occasions.

Keegan again surprised the world of football when he returned to England to play for Southampton in 1980. With another 37 goals in League games to his credit, he then moved to Newcastle United, where he scored another 48 times in 78 League encounters. By now a Newcastle legend, as well as an Anfield hero, in 1984 he quit in favour of a Spanish golf course. He took over as manager at St James's Park in 1992, then shocked Newcastle by resigning in 1997.

Football had not however seen the last of Kevin Keegan. He returned to the game as manager of a resurgent Fulham, and was then appointed to the top job: manager of the England side, early in 1999. The appointment promised much, but Keegan himself felt he was not quite up to it. Following a 1-0 defeat by Germany in a World Cup qualifying game in October 2000, he resigned in dramatic fashion. His record of Played 18, Won 7, Drawn 7 and Lost 4 was actually not very impressive.

Following a spell as manager of Manchester City, a post from which he resigned in March 2005, it seems that Kevin Keegan may now be lost to the game. He may be, but on the other hand…

ABOVE Kevin Keegan is congratulated after scoring the first goal in the 1974 FA Cup Final against Newcastle United

LEFT Keegan takes the ball past Dave Clement of Queens Park Rangers

Kennedys

THE COMBINED TALENTS OF RAY and Alan Kennedy ensured their shared surname remained on Liverpool's team sheet from 1974 to 1985. Unrelated north-easterners, they each played a major role in the club's success as well as representing England. They also combined on the field in memorable fashion to win the 1981 European Cup.

Midfielder Ray, born 28 July 1951, had already achieved the Double with Arsenal in 1970-71 when he became Bill

RIGHT Ray Kennedy closes down Gerry Francis of QPR

BELOW In it goes! Ray Kennedy salutes Kenny Dalglish's winning goal as Liverpool win the European Cup in 1978

Shankly's last signing at Anfield. His form had been in the doldrums for some time before new boss Bob Paisley switched him from attack to midfield and confidence was restored.

Liverpool won the League title in 1975-76 and he went on to play a major part in the successes to come. Three European Cup winners' medals, one UEFA Cup, four further Championship titles and one League Cup were won along with 17 caps for England in a prolific period for Liverpool Football Club as the midfield of Souness, Case, McDermott and Kennedy swept aside all before them.

In 1982, he transferred to John Toshack's Swansea, but things did not work out and he left for Hartlepool before trying his hand at management abroad. In 1985 Ray Kennedy was diagnosed as suffering from Parkinson's Disease and has since spent his time raising public awareness of the illness and dealing with his own health and personal problems.

Alan Kennedy (born 31 August 1954) was an attacking full-back who joined from first club Newcastle in 1978.

He will be remembered for his goal against Real Madrid that won the European Cup Final in Paris in 1981. With the game poised at 1-1, Alan ran into Ray's throw, smashed the ball past keeper Agustin with just six minutes remaining.

Three years later in the same competition, he secured the Treble for Liverpool with the decisive penalty in a shoot-out with Roma in Rome. The capture

of the European Cup, League Championship and League Cup led to Kennedy being selected for England by Bobby Robson that summer.

He was lauded by the Kop, who nicknamed him 'Barney Rubble' because he was everyone's favourite sidekick and regularly bailed the Reds out of trouble with his well-timed interventions. In 1985, however, 31-year-old Kennedy was replaced in the Liverpool side by Jim Beglin and left for his home-town club of Sunderland.

With Liverpool he had won every major honour, except the FA Cup, more than once. He was a tough-tackling defender, but when the time came to counter-attack he had the pace and eye for an opening that proved invaluable.

ABOVE Alan Kennedy kisses the European Cup after scoring the decisive goal in the 1981 Final

BELOW LEFT Alan Kennedy in action

Kit

PRIOR TO THE BILL SHANKLY ERA,
Liverpool had worn red shirts and
white shorts since their original blue
and white quarters were discarded in
the 1898 season. But just as Leeds
rival Don Revie boosted his side's
fortunes by adopting Real Madrid's all-
white, so Shankly hit upon the idea of
wearing all red.

It's said that the decision was made
after being drawn against Anderlecht in
the second round of the club's first
European Cup campaign in 1964-1965.
Captain Ron Yeats, he said, would look
even bigger if he wore red shorts, while
Ian St John suggested red socks to complete the now legendary all-red
Liverpool kit.

There have been several cosmetic
tweaks over the years, most notably yellow pinstripes of the mid 1980s and the

LEFT Roy Evans displays Liverpool's new team strip in 1994

BELOW Fernando Morientes poses with his new kit, 2005

Adidas 'three stripe' adornments that followed, while the liver bird badge with the LFC letters below it came off the white oval background to be embroidered directly on the shirt. It was then surrounded by a shield.

Away kits have varied from green through white to grey, and, like the home kit, have been dominated by sponsors' logos. Yet these have been mercifully few. While the 1980s saw Crown Paints splashed on red shirts, Carlsberg, have been the club's sponsors since 1992, and have signed up until 2007.

Kop

THE BANKED TERRACE BEHIND
the goal was first named the Spion Kop
in 1906 after the site of a battle in the
Second Boer War where British forces
suffered particularly heavy losses. Kop is
Afrikaans for 'hill'. At its height, the
Kop was one of the largest single tier
stands in the world and could hold
28,000 spectators, but the Taylor Report
that had followed the tragedy at

BELOW Fans in the
Kop celebrate another
Liverpool victory

Hillsborough meant that the days of
watching top-class football from standing terraces were numbered.

So it was inevitable that a tear would be shed as the bulldozers moved in to prepare the Kop for all-seater status after the last home game against Norwich on 30 April 1994. Yet with Liverpool families having suffered that tragic loss, no-one needed telling it had to be done.

When it was completely rebuilt as an all-seater stand in 1994, the Kop's capacity shrunk to 12,409. Legend has it that the fans could suck the ball into the goal if Liverpool were playing towards that end. Many other grounds boast a kop, but this is the original and best with a capital K.

ABOVE Bill Shankly receives the acclaim of the Kop after Liverpool clinched the Football League Championship in 1973

LEFT Supporters lining up outside the Kop for the victory parade through the streets of Liverpool, in celebration of clinching the European trophy, 2005

Lawler

BILL SHANKLY INHERITED a side which needed a stronger and more effective defence, and for this reason Chris Lawler was to become a key member of his side. Born in Liverpool on 20 October 1943, Lawler's first ambition was fulfilled when he signed for his home town club as a 17 year-old. Strong, and very quick moving for a six-footer, Lawler occupied the right-back position with distinction for many years. His turn of speed also meant that he was capable of running down the flank and crossing the ball for others to score, although in his 406 League appearances for Liverpool he himself netted on 41 occasions.

Chris Lawler played just four times for England, but had the gods been with him he might have featured in many more internationals. As it was, he gave sterling service to his chosen club before moving to Portsmouth to play under former colleague Ian St John in 1975. At Fratton Park he made a further 36 League appearances before ending his playing career at Stockport County – where he scored three times in another 36 games. Later, a testimonial match was held for him at Anfield, which was attended by 20,000 loyal Liverpudlians.

Lawrence

BORN IN AYRSHIRE ON 14 MAY 1940, Tommy Lawrence moved with his parents to Warrington before becoming one of the many Scottish born footballers to earn fame and modest fortune with Bill Shankly's Liverpool. Having shown promise as an amateur goalkeeper, he went along to Anfield for a trial, signed professional at 17, and spent the next few years playing junior and reserve team football, finally making his League debut in 1962.

Lawrence measured 5ft 11in and presented a somewhat stocky appearance, but this did not prevent him from becoming an excellent custodian. Liverpool fans affectionately called him the 'Flying Pig' and, rather like his Anfield descendant Grobbelaar, he became famous for racing out of his area to hoof the ball upfield. Given that the Liverpool defence was so accomplished at the time, this may well have arisen from boredom.

During his seven-and-a-half seasons of first-team football with Liverpool, Lawrence missed just five games, but he earned just three caps for Scotland – a

country not generally noted for the excellence of its goalkeepers. Lawrence was exceptionally loyal to his club and did not really want to move to Tranmere Rovers when his transfer was arranged in 1971. He ended his playing days there, until his retirement in 1973, after which he worked at a wire factory in Warrington.

ABOVE Tommy Lawrence in thoughtful mood, 1970

Lawrenson

MARK LAWRENSON WAS born in Preston on 2 June 1957. He played for North End, and then Brighton, but in his early years his abilities as a defender hardly set the footballing world alight. He was however targeted by Bob Paisley and, in 1981, moved to Liverpool for a surprisingly large £900,000 fee.

RIGHT Lawrenson heads the ball during the European Cup Final against Roma, 1984

BELOW Mark Lawrenson on the ball

As ever, Paisley knew what he was doing. Lawrenson was dogged by injury in his later years, but between 1981 and 1986 his pace, timing and overall footballing intelligence meant that he contributed in no small measure towards the frequent lifting of silverware at Anfield.

Lawrenson won 38 caps for his chosen country, the Republic of Ireland, but many in England wished he had chosen the Three Lions instead. His Mum, who collected every article and programme in which Mark Lawrenson's name appeared, would perhaps have been even more proud of her son.

When Achilles tendon trouble ended his playing days, Lawrenson embarked upon a managerial career, but it proved less than successful. He was at Oxford and Peterborough United before moving to Newcastle as defensive coach (a job which nobody envied). He is now a noted television pundit, where his Achilles tendon is safe from further injury unless Alan Hansen gives him a surreptitious kick under the table.

League Cup

THE FOOTBALL LEAGUE CUP, otherwise known as Hardaker's Folly after the man whose vision it was, could never have been termed a runaway success. Indeed, Liverpool and Everton initially declined the invitation to enter, in common with other leading clubs, considering it less as a potential crowd-puller as unwanted extra fixtures. The introduction of a one-legged Wembley final and a place in Europe for the winner changed all that, and it was this that brought the first meeting of Merseyside's top two teams on Wembley's hallowed turf. Even the first Charity Shield the pair had contested, in 1966, had been played at Goodison.

The League Cup Final of 1984, was the match Merseyside had waited nearly a century for... but the result in the pouring rain was an anti-climactic scoreless draw. The lack of goals was probably not surprising, since the teams boasted two of the meanest defences in the League. No-one wanted to lose this game, so the result was perhaps the best one. And the combined chants of 'Merseyside' that rose from the terraces confirmed that this had been no ordinary fixture, these were no ordinary supporters.

The replay was staged four days later at Maine Road, 52,089 Merseysiders making the pilgrimage down the East Lancs Road. Maybe coats could have been put down in Stanley Park... It was always likely that one goal would be enough to decide things, and it was an undistinguished Graeme Souness effort that skidded past Southall to settle the destination of the silverware.

BELOW The victorious Liverpool team that won the League Cup in 1984

Spurs and Man U were the victims in an unparalleled 'four in a row'. All four games, interestingly, went to extra time, while dispatching West Ham had required a Villa Park replay after a 1-1 Wembley draw.

The Reds' 1987 visit to Wembley saw them lose 2-1 to Arsenal, but normal service was resumed in 1995 as Bolton were dispatched by a Steve McManaman brace. There followed three visits to the Millennium Stadium, Cardiff, a win on penalties against Birmingham City in 2001 followed by a record seventh win in 2003 against Manchester United and defeat to Chelsea in 2005.

The Reds' first visit to a League Cup Final six years earlier ended in replay defeat to Brian Clough's Nottingham Forest, but the Everton fixture was their fourth Final in succession. West Ham,

Lest We Forget

TWO TRAGEDIES IN 1985 AND 1989 will forever be remembered by not only Liverpool supporters but football as a whole.

On 29 May 1985, when England, and much of Europe, was in the grip of so-called 'football hooliganism', Liverpool were playing in the European Cup Final against Juventus. The venue was the Heysel Stadium in Brussels, a crumbling edifice which was palpably unsuitable for the purpose, and which had in fact been condemned as a venue for major matches. Liverpool had objected that a neutral section of the ground set aside for Belgian fans would lead to both sets of supporters buying tickets off touts, and such warnings proved well-founded as this area filled with Italian fans.

Fighting broke out during the game, a wall collapsed and carnage resulted. As the Liverpool website states, "Instead of leaving Brussels having seen our team lift a fifth European Cup, Liverpool supporters travelled back to England having witnessed the deaths of 38 Italians and one Belgian." English teams were immediately banned from European competition for six years.

When Liverpool and Juventus were drawn together in the Champions League in 2005, their first meeting since the Heysel tragedy, many former players and some supporters attempted to heal the wounds with symbolic ceremonies and acts of friendship.

BELOW A rather subdued crowd watches Liverpool play Juventus at Heysel, 1985

LEST WE FORGET

ABOVE In 1999, 96 front row seats at the Leppings Lane End of Hillsborough, where fans lost their lives 10 years ago, were roped off and each had a rose placed on it, to remember the 1989 disaster

At Hillsborough, on 15th April 1989, 96 Liverpool fans waiting to watch their side contest a Cup semi-final against Nottingham Forest would lose their lives. The tragedy threw any event on the pitch into perspective and made a mockery of the saying attributed to Bill Shankly that "football's not a matter of life and death…it's more important than that."

Once again, the event was witnessed by millions via their television screens.

On this occasion, it was Liverpool supporters who were suffocated or crushed to death, when the police allowed too many people to enter the Leppings Lane end of the ground. Even before the game kicked off, it was clear to many that there was severe overcrowding at one end of the stadium, but still the fans piled in.

By the time the referee abandoned the game after just six minutes, people were climbing over the barriers and onto the pitch, in an effort to escape being crushed. Some of them made it. Ninety-five did not (one fan survived and died later). It was a disaster of unparalleled proportions, and it would lead to revolutionary changes at football grounds throughout the country.

The dead of Hillsborough are commemorated by a memorial next to the Shankly Gates at Anfield. Its eternal flame signifies that their memory will live forever. Sheffield Wednesday, after years of lobbying by relatives, erected a memorial at the site of the tragedy in 1999.

Liddell

THESE DAYS BILLY LIDDELL perhaps appears to be something of an unsung hero, although older Liverpool supporters will remember the 'Flying Scotsman' with deep affection. Born in Dunfermline on 10 January 1922, he was a speedy left-winger with a remarkable appetite for scoring goals. Although Liverpool won the League championship in 1947, and reached the FA Cup Final in 1950, Liddell's side was mainly a Second Division outfit during his time at Anfield. Honours were therefore few and far between.

It was the duty of the old-fashioned winger to make goals for others. This Liddell duly did but, in his 495 Liverpool League games, he scored a remarkable 216 goals himself. Between 1946 and 1958, he averaged 38 League games per season. He also played 28 times for Scotland, where his goal tally was restricted to just half a dozen.

'King Billy' was one of football's gentlemen. He seldom committed a foul and showed true remorse when he occasionally did. He played until he was 38, but in the days when footballers were paid nothing like today's inflated wages, he prepared himself for life after football: while still playing, he qualified as an accountant. Billy Liddell died, aged 78, in 2001.

LEFT Billy Liddell pictured in 1949

Larry Lloyd (left), assisted by Kevin Keegan, competes with Jack Charlton (right) and Paul Madeley of Leeds in a 1972 match

Lloyd

BORN ON 6 OCTOBER 1948, 20-year-old Larry Lloyd made the move north from Bristol Rovers to Liverpool in April 1969. Bought by Bill Shankly to take over from the mighty Ron Yeats, Lloyd didn't disappoint. Like big Ron, the incoming centre-half was from the old school of defending, commanding in the air and strong in the tackle. He made his first team debut at Dundalk in the old Fairs Cup in September 1969 and was selected for eight League games that season as he was eased into the Anfield set-up.

Lloyd missed only a couple of League games the following season and chalked up an FA Cup Final appearance only for Arsenal to win the contest in extra time. After a close run for the League title in 1971-72 Lloyd enjoyed his best season for Liverpool the following year, being ever-present as the Reds pulled off a memorable League and UEFA Cup double. In fact he topped off the European campaign by scoring the all important third goal in the first leg against Borussia Moenchengladbach. The Germans pulled two goals back in the return match, but Liverpool held on.

In August 1974 he moved on to Coventry City but it was Brian Clough who relaunched his career by taking him to Nottingham Forest in 1976. There he won another League title and two European Cup winners' medals plus two League Cup winners' medals.

Managers

1892-96	WE Barclay	1928-36	George Patterson
1896-1915	Tom Watson	1936-51	George Kay
1920-23	David Ashworth	1951-56	Don Welsh
1923-28	Matt McQueen	1956-59	Phil Taylor

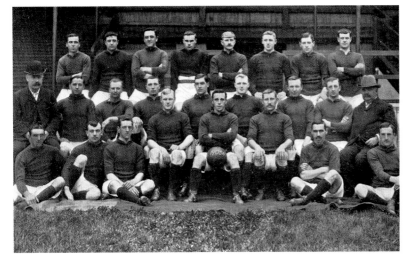

ABOVE A 1932 Liverpool team photo, with George Patterson (bottom row far left)

LEFT The Liverpool team pictured in 1905 with manager Tom Watson (middle row far right)

MANAGERS

BELOW A shot from 1969, which includes five past managers of the club. Roy Evans (back row third from left), Ronnie Moran (2nd row on left) Bob Paisley and Bill Shankly (third row on left) and Joe Fagan (third row second from right)

1959-74	Bill Shankly
1974-83	Bob Paisley
1983-85	Joe Fagan
1985-91	Kenny Dalglish
1991-94	Graeme Souness
1994-98	Roy Evans
1998-2004	Gerard Houllier
2004-to date	Rafael Benitez

McDermott

BORN ON 8 DECEMBER 1951 in nearby Kirkby, Terry McDermott worshipped Liverpool as a child but it was from Newcastle United that he arrived for £160,000 in 1974, just six months after Liverpool had beaten the Magpies in the FA Cup Final. His first-team appearances over the coming two seasons were sporadic but once Bob Paisley restructured the side he became a regular in midfield.

McDermott served the club well over his eight seasons at Anfield, a period that netted 11 major honours including three European Cups, in the first of which he played an important part by scoring a brilliant opening goal in the 3-1 win over Moenchengladbach in Rome. He also achieved the rare feat of winning both the Football Writers' and the PFA Player of the Year awards in 1980.

Despite the fact that he was a fine ball-winner and innovative playmaker McDermott always felt insecure in the team and it was in the 1982-83 season he returned to Newcastle after an indifferent finale to a glorious career at Anfield. At St James' Park he became assistant manager to Kevin Keegan as Sir John Hall poured millions into a rebuilding programme. He has since worked there as a member of the backroom staff with former Anfield favourites Kenny Dalglish and Graeme Souness, while his son is a first-team fringe player for Fulham.

OPPOSITE LEFT Liverpool manager Kenny Dalglish, pictured with coaches (and future managers) Ronnie Moran and Roy Evans, celebrating becoming League Champions in 1990

LEFT McDermott pictured in 1981

BELOW Terry McDermott takes the ball past Trevor Brooking of West Ham United, 1977

McMahon

FORMER EVERTONIAN STEVE McMahon (born 20 August 1961) crossed Stanley Park in a roundabout way via Aston Villa in 1985, having

Steve McMahon beats Michael Phelan of Manchester United in the 1990 Charity Shield

enhanced his reputation as a battling midfielder during his two years in the Midlands. He became Kenny Dalglish's first signing, and the £350,000 was well spent. Graeme Souness's departure for Italy had left a gap in Liverpool's midfield that had never been properly filled.

In McMahon, Dalglish saw a man equally capable of the bonecrunching tackle or defence-splitting pass, someone who could bring bite and subtlety in equal measure, a combination sorely lacking in the existing Liverpool midfield.

Playing in perhaps the last great Liverpool side, McMahon secured League Championship and FA Cup winning medals, not to mention 17 caps for England (he was selected in Bobby Robson's World Cup squad for Italia '90.) The irony of Mahon's Anfield career is the fact it was curtailed by the very man he was bought to replace – Graeme Souness. After six seasons at the club, McMahon was shipped out to Manchester City for £900,000; he was sorely missed. He later began a management career in promising style, winning the Second Division championship for Swindon Town after it seemed the Wiltshire club was in freefall, but later efforts with the likes of Blackpool failed to bear fruit and he'd appeared to have settled, as have so many ex-Reds, for life as a media commentator, before surprisingly heading for Australia and taking over as head coach of Perth Glory in February 2005.

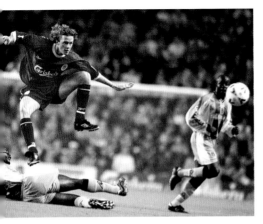

McManaman

ON HIS DEBUT IN DECEMBER 1990, floppy-maned Steve McManaman (born 11 February 1972) was hailed as a winger with unlimited talent. Born on Merseyside, McManaman's willowy build belied a powerful turn of pace. Though his goalscoring record was disappointing, a spectacular brace against Bolton Wanderers in the 1995 Coca-Cola Cup Final were rated among the finest goals seen at Wembley in recent years.

After an impressive debut season ending in an FA Cup win against Sunderland, McManaman lost his way during the next campaign, but his form at club level returned as he forged a potent partnership with another former apprentice, Robbie Fowler, their burgeoning understanding one of the real plus points of some underachieving seasons.

McManaman's impressive displays saw him claim an England place, making his debut in November 1994, but having established himself as a regular he fell out with then-boss Glenn Hoddle and never had a look-in under Eriksson. Made club captain after turning down a move to Barcelona, he had played 364 games (66 goals) in red when he became the first major Liverpool player to leave Anfield on a Bosman free transfer when he joined Real Madrid in the summer of 1999.

He scored spectacularly in the European Cup Final against Valencia to end a successful first season at the Bernabeu but he increasingly found himself marginalised and returned to the Premiership with Kevin Keegan's Manchester City in 2003. Injury blighted his Maine Road stay and he was freed in 2005, age 33.

LEFT Steve McManaman leaps over a Coventry City player at Anfield,1998

BELOW McManaman runs with the ball for Liverpool

Melwood

LIVERPOOL FOOTBALL CLUB'S
training ground, Melwood, has
been used by the club since the 50's
when it was bought from
St Francis Xavier RC school. The
name came from two of the priests,
Father Melling and
Father Woodcock, who
taught the boys football.

A wooden pavilion
was replaced by a brick
one otherwise little
was done to develop
Melwood until January
2001 when the Millennium
Pavilion started to take
shape. This included a press
room, staff offices for manager and coaches, and
expanded changing facili-
ties. On the health and fitness side, a gymnasium
(split into two areas and
computer controlled) is
accompanied by a physio-
therapy room and small
hydrotherapy pool which
can be used in all weathers.

There are several full size pitches at
Melwood, while a small covered area
lets players train on a synthetic surface
when the weather is unfavourable. In
the old days security was lax, but nowa-
days each player has his own key card
that allows them entry. They arrive at
9.30am for the daily morning sessions
that run from 10-12am, augmented by
occasional evening training. Most players will sign autographs before or after
training or pose for a photograph with
fans who travel from around the world
to see their heroes.

Merseyside Final

THE 1980S BROUGHT THREE CUP Final meetings between Liverpool and Everton, the League Cup in 1984 and FA Cup in 1986 and 1989. There were those who wondered why a local contest should have to transport itself 200 miles south to be decided, but half of the city enjoyed taking the day trip to Wembley (and another to Maine Road, after the League Cup Final was drawn.)

The first FA Cup Final in '86 was won 3-1 by Liverpool, giving them the League and Cup Double for what was only the third time by any team in the 20th century. Though Gary Lineker opened the scoring, it was man of the match Ian Rush who equalised before setting up Craig Johnston to put the Reds ahead. A second from Rushie rubbed salt in the wound.

A different kind of wound, Hillsborough, overshadowed the second FA Cup meeting in 1989. Some would say the game re-established some sense of normality to a city that had, perhaps, taken the Shankly aphorism about football being more important than life or death too literally until then. The match went into extra time at 1-1, at which point Ian Rush, the hero three years earlier, came off the bench to score two more goals, the first equalised by McCall, to add to John Aldridge's early strike and establish a winning 3-2 lead.

Some from the blue side of the city resented the fact that somehow they were expected to roll over and let Liverpool win it 'for the fans'. But a hard-fought five-goal thriller was, for the neutral at least, a footballing showcase and a great advert for the city.

BELOW The team captains Ronnie Whelan and Kevin Ratcliffe of Everton shake hands before the FA Cup Final in 1989

Molby

A SUPERB PASSER AND POSSESSOR of a lethal shot, Jan Molby (born 4 July 1963) started his playing career with his hometown club, Kolding, in Denmark before moving to Ajax Amsterdam.

RIGHT Molby controls the ball for Liverpool

BELOW Jan Molby charges with the ball against Newcastle in 1985

The 'Great Dane' was signed by Joe Fagan in August 1984 for £200,000 in the wake of Graeme Souness's departure. Molby's wonderful range of measured and incisive passing fitted the Liverpool bill perfectly, although his Anfield career was subsequently blighted by weight problems and a spell in prison for a driving offence. If Molby was very handy at free-kicks he was deadly at penalties, netting 40 out of 42 for the Reds, even

helping himself to a hat-trick of spot-kicks against Coventry City in the League Cup in November 1986. In that season, Liverpool claimed the League and FA Cup Double – rivals Everton were runners-up in both competitions – and the Danish international was instrumental in all three FA Cup Final goals as Liverpool recovered from going a goal behind to win 3-1. Prolific goalscorer Ian Rush, in particular, was one of a number of strikers to benefit from Molby's 'assists'.

Further League titles were clinched in 1988 and 1990 and another FA Cup success followed in 1992. Molby was released by Liverpool in February 1996 when he joined Swansea City as player-manager, but was afforded a testimonial for his 10-plus years at Anfield. He has since enjoyed a less stellar management career with Kidderminster (twice) and Hull.

Morientes

FOR SPANISH STRIKER FERNANDO Morientes (born 5 April 1976), his European appearances for Real Madrid restricted him to cheering on the sidelines as his new club picked up the ultimate prize. He quit the Bernabeu after a season on loan at Monaco, but was still rated one of the continent's most dangerous frontman and undoubtedly has a part to play in Rafa Benitez's future plans.

His career began in 1993 at Albacete, and a haul of 38 goals in two seasons with Real Zaragoza brought him to Real Madrid's attention. His first season saw them lift the European Cup in 1998, while March that year saw him score on his Spain debut.

Two years later came another European Cup. In 2001 Morientes won his first league title with Real, but missed the tail-end of the season due to injury. Back to form and fitness in 2002, he scored five in Real's 7-0 win over Las Palmas in February and ended the season as top scorer with 18 league goals. He also won a third European Cup medal with Real's 2-1 win over Bayer Leverkusen, but his three-goal World Cup quest ended in the quarter-finals.

Frustratingly cup-tied for his new club's Champions League triumph, Morientes did play in the 2005 Super Cup victory against CSKA Moscow. The 2005-06 season was not spectacular and he returned to Spain and Valencia for around £3 million.

LEFT Fernando Morientes celebrates scoring Liverpool's first goal against Portsmouth in 2005

BELOW Morientes takes control for Liverpool

Neal

THE EVER-DEPENDABLE PHIL Neal (born 20 February 1951) had racked up almost 200 League appearances for Northampton Town before he became Bob Paisley's first signing in October 1974 and was pitched into the Liverpool way of things immediately with a derby encounter at Goodison Park.

It was the springboard to a glittering career as Neal went on to become one of the most decorated footballers in the English game. So much so that it's easier to name the one competition – the FA Cup – in which he did not claim a winners' medal! Neal helped Liverpool to the League championship in his first full season – 1975-76 – the first of eight such triumphs. League Cup winners' medals were garnered in four successive seasons, 1981-84, while in European competitions Neal and Liverpool were UEFA Cup winners in 1976 and European Cup champions in 1977, 1978, 1981 and 1984.

Although a midfielder with Northampton, he made the right-back position his own at Anfield – and for England, gaining 50 caps – although he was able to play anywhere along the back four. He took over penalty-taking duties from Kevin Keegan during the 1975-76 season and it was Neal's spot-kick that sealed the club's first European Cup success in 1977 after Keegan had been felled. He was also on the mark, this time from open play, in the 1984 final before reverting to his role as spot-kick king as Liverpool won the match on penalties.

New Stadium

IN 2003, LIVERPOOL PREPARED A planning application to build a stadium in Stanley Park, just a few hundred yards from Anfield. The current stadium would only be able to expand it to a maximum of 55,000 seats. The original plan was for a ground with 70,000 seats, but this was later reduced by 10,000 due to cost considerations.

Liverpool's original plan was to swap the Stanley Park land they'd build on for the present ground, the current site becoming part of the park. That was deemed unacceptable by English Heritage and CABE (Commission for Architecture and the Built Environment) who wanted to see some development rather than "more windswept open space". A series of ideas was then developed in conjunction with local people to create a joint venture between club, city and community that might include cafés/restaurants, offices, high quality open space and an open-air market in an Anfield Plaza.

The plan was for the new ground's opening to coincide with the city's Year as European Capital of Culture in 2008. With the takeover of the club by Americans George Gillett and Tom Hicks, there was speculation on a capacity increase to 80,000. A revised completion date of 2009 was announced in April 2007.

A modern stadium within Stanley Park will allow Liverpool to compete with the Manchester Uniteds and Arsenals. It seems likely, however, that its name will be sold off to the highest bidder, so 'New Anfield' appears a nonstarter – as is a ground-share with Everton, who are also looking to relocate.

TOP AND BOTTOM
An artist's impression
of the new stadium

Nicol

STEVE NICOL FORMED PART OF the backbone of the Liverpool side throughout the 1980s. Initially a defender, he later occupied midfield positions and altogether he made 343 League appearances in a Liverpool shirt, scoring on 36 occasions.

Nicol, born in Irvine, Scotland on 11 December 1961, began his career with Ayr United and signed on at Anfield in 1981 for a fee of £300,000. His contribution to the Liverpool side of the 1980s, while not forgotten, is probably not as well remembered as that of the players with whom he starred. He developed a very useful partnership with John Barnes and, while not building a reputation as a prolific goalscorer himself, he did on one occasion score a hat-trick against Newcastle at St James's Park, and had a fourth goal disallowed in the same game. In 1989, he was voted the PFA's Footballer of the Year.

Having won 27 caps for Scotland, and having played for his country in the 1986 World Cup finals, Nicol left Anfield in 1994. He moved to Notts County as player-coach for a brief period, and then went on to David Pleat's Sheffield Wednesday and to Doncaster Rovers. Later, he took up coaching in the United States, where he still lives.

Owen

BORN IN CHESTER ON 14 December 1979, Michael supported rivals Everton as a youngster but was spotted playing schools football in Hawarden and signed for Liverpool as an apprentice. His first team debut was a scoring one in May 1997, when he came on as substitute against Wimbledon.

The following season saw him joint top scorer in the Premier League, with international recognition coming against Chile in February 1998 when he became the youngest player to have represented his country all century. That year's World Cup brought memorable substitute performances in both the initial group matches and against Romania. A spectacular individual goal against Argentina confirmed him as an international force and successor to David Beckham as pin-up and fan favourite. He has since played in and scored at the 2000 and 2004 European Championships and 2002 World Cup.

Having played 297 times for his first club, scoring 158 goals, Michael Owen moved to Real Madrid in 2004 and, having been an automatic choice for club and country, found himself on the bench more often than not. Ironically, Liverpool were crowned the European Champions while the Spaniards suffered a trophyless season, but a summer 2005 move to Newcastle United meant English football hadn't seen the last of Michael Owen.

ABOVE Owen passes the ball for Liverpool

Paisley

BORN ON 23 JANUARY 1919, BOB Paisley had become part of the Anfield furniture when he was chosen to succeed Bill Shankly as Liverpool manager in 1974. His playing career in red had been unremarkable, missing out on the FA Cup Final in 1950, but as a manager he would become world-famous.

His first season, 1974-75, was a barren one. But when the likes of Phil Neal and Terry McDermott had bedded in alongside local lad Jimmy Case and courageous Emlyn Hughes the League title was there for the taking in 1976. Next would come the European Cup, the biggest prize of all, and as in '73 Borussia Moenchengladbach were the opposition, beaten 3-1 this time in Rome. The Reds also retained the Championship at home after a run of 16 games without defeat took them clear of Manchester City, though Kevin Keegan's decision to leave English football for Hamburg was a bitter blow.

Yet even he was replaceable in Paisley's Red machine – and Kenny Dalglish, prised from Glasgow giants Celtic for a record £440,000, would make just as big a mark. He slotted into a team in transition, stalwarts like Tommy Smith and John Toshack giving way to the likes of Alan Hansen and David Johnson.

The one disappointment of 1976-77 for Bob Paisley was missing out on the

FA Cup – a win against Manchester United, the previous year's runners-up, in the Final would have brought up a unique 'Treble', but it was not to be. With Dalglish in Keegan's Number 7 shirt, a draw was obtained against United in the Charity Shield, but retaining the European Cup was the priority and that was done with a Dalglish goal against Belgian champs Bruges at Wembley,

Another Championship in 1978-79 was achieved with only four games lost and 16 goals conceded – no wonder keeper Ray Clemence was an England squad regular! The title was retained in 1979-80, though the League Cup would remain an impossible dream until 1981. Then they just couldn't stop winning it – four victories in as many years! Another European Cup, the third in five years, was achieved thanks to a rare goal from Alan Kennedy in 1981.

Bob Paisley carried his last trophy back to the boardroom in May 1983 as Liverpool retained the League title. The respect in which he was held was immense, and when he went up Wembley's 39 steps to receive the League Cup that March he was the first manager ever to be awarded such an accolade. Three European Cups, six League titles, three Milk (League) Cups and a UEFA Cup had made him uniquely successful, a fact the Paisley gates at Anfield celebrates. Bob died in 1996 but, like Bill Shankly, will never be forgotten.

ABOVE Bob Paisley with the League Championship trophy, pictured in 1983

Quotes

RIGHT Roy Evans shouts instructions to the Liverpool team

LIVERPOOL FC HAS ALWAYS BEEN populated by people with opinions. Here are just some of them.

"We knew that all other things being equal, like skill, tactics and run of the ball, it was fitness that would count in the end. So we kept at 100% at all times, and it paid us. We have found that there is more satisfaction in a good win than there is in a pint or a cigarette packet." **Roger Hunt**

"If you're in the penalty area and don't know what to do with the ball, put it in the net and we'll discuss the options later." **Bob Paisley**

"We've got a lot of Cockneys in the team, but really, it doesn't matter where they're from – we're all playing for Liverpool." **Robbie Fowler**

"I've been on this planet for 45 years, and have supported Liverpool for 42 of them." **Roy Evans**

"Sometimes I feel I'm hardly wanted in this Liverpool team. If I get two or three saves to make, I've had a busy day." **Ray Clemence**

"At Liverpool we never accept second best." **Kenny Dalglish**

"Liverpool are magic, Everton are tragic." **Emlyn Hughes**

"Mind you, I've been here during the bad times too – one year we came second." **Bob Paisley**

"(Bob Paisley) could tell if someone was injured and what the problem was just by watching them walk a few paces. He was never boastful but had great football knowledge. I owe Bob more than I owe anybody else in the game. There will never be another like him." **Kenny Dalglish**

"See this shirt – I'm keeping it because it will be one of my most treasured possessions. It's only just beginning to sink in that it's all over for me as a Liverpool player." **Ian Rush**

"Shanks was the father figure but Roger Hunt was something special. It might sound daft but just picking up his sweaty kit gave me satisfaction." **Phil Thompson**

"The Liverpool philosophy is simple, and is based on total belief. Maybe that has been the key to Liverpool's consistency. We were taught to go out there, play our own game and fear no one." **Phil Neal**

"Liverpool without European football is like a banquet without wine." **Roy Evans**

"Everything seemed to go like clockwork at Liverpool, as though nobody was in charge." **Mark Lawrenson**

"There's no noise like the Anfield noise – and I love it!" **Ian St John**

"We don't have any splits here. The players' country is Liverpool Football Club and their language is football." **Gerard Houllier**

"My life is my work. My work is my life." **Bill Shankly**

"I can let the team do the talking for me." **Bob Paisley**

"I'd kick my own brother if necessary... it's what being a professional footballer is all about." **Steve McMahon**

BELOW
Steve McMahon controls the ball for Liverpool

"I said to Kevin (Keegan), 'I'll go near post' and he replied, 'No, just go for the ball." **Tommy Smith**

"It's best being a striker. If you miss five then score the winner, you're a hero. The goalkeeper can play a blinder, then let one in… and he's a villain." **Ian Rush**

"Nobody likes being criticised, particularly by players who will be in Disneyland this summer on their holidays rather than the World Cup in Japan**." Phil Thompson responding to criticism from Frank de Boer of Barcelona who said Liverpool were boring**

"Bill was so strong it was unbelievable. You couldn't shake him off the ball. It didn't matter where he was playing, though I suppose his best position was outside-left. He could go round you, past you, or even straight through you sometimes!" **Bob Paisley on Billy Liddell**

"I go by records and Bob Paisley is the No 1 manager ever!" **Alan Hansen**

"Liverpool wouldn't be the club it is today without Bill Shankly and Bob Paisley and the players who played there. When I first went there it was a typical Second Division ground and look at it now!" **Ian Callaghan**

"I may have left Liverpool but the city and club will always be part of me." **Kenny Dalglish**

On awaiting Everton's arrival for a derby game at Anfield, Bill Shankly gave a box of toilet rolls to the door-man and said: "Give them these when they arrive – they'll need them!"

"He's better than Platini, certainly better than Rummenigge and Maradona. For me he is the greatest footballer in the world." **Graeme Souness on Kenny Dalglish**

"I notice a former captain of ours said recently that this squad is so good that we don't need a manager. I took this as a great compliment. He must have changed his mind since leaving as he said at the time that Phil Thompson and I would drag the club down. On that point I suppose he was right - we dragged the club down to Cardiff three times in the last 10 months." **Gerard Houllier referring to comments made by Paul Ince**

"The only thing I fear is missing an open goal in front of the Kop. I would die if that were to happen. When they start singing 'You'll Never Walk Alone' my eyes start to water. There have been times when I've actually been crying while I've been playing." **Kevin Keegan**

"I will never forget today and I want to thank all the fans who gave me such a great ovation. They were immense. I thought I would get a decent reception but that surpassed all my wildest dreams. That sort of ovation is normally reserved for players who have won European Cups for a club. It was a brilliant day and it was nice to hear the Kop's humour at its best again when

they were telling me to go back to Coventry." **Gary Mc-Allister after his last game for Liverpool at Anfield**

"See this shirt - I'm keeping it because it will be one of my most treasured possessions. It's only just beginning to sink in that it's all over for me as a Liverpool player." **Ian Rush**

"With Crouch, with (Anthony) Le Tallec, or with (Fernando) Morientes and Cisse I will have more problems - but I like these kind of problems." **Rafa Benitez**

Avi Cohen to Kenny Dalglish on the day that Cohen joined the club: "You, me, same."
Dalglish, perplexed, just nodded. But when the next day Cohen said the same thing. Dalglish said, "What are you talking about, Avi?" "You, me, same. Both learn English."

Records

APPEARANCES

Most first team appearances
Ian Callaghan (857)

Most League appearances
Ian Callaghan (640)

Most FA Cup appearances
Ian Callaghan (79)

Most League Cup appearances
Ian Rush (78)

Most European appearances
Ian Callaghan (89)

Oldest player
Ted Doig, 41 years and 165 days v Newcastle United (A) 11 April 1908

Youngest player
Max Thompson, 17 years and 129 days v Tottenham Hotspur (A) 8 May 1974

Most seasons as an ever-present
Phil Neal (9)

Most consecutive appearances
Phil Neal (417) 23 October 1976 to 24 September 1983

Longest-serving player
Elisha Scott – 21 years and 52 days, 1913-34

Oldest debutant
Ted Doig, 37 years and 307 days v Burton U (H) 1 September 1904

GOALS

Most first team goals
Ian Rush (346)

Most League goals
Roger Hunt (245)

Most FA Cup goals
Ian Rush (39)

Most League Cup goals
Ian Rush (48)

Most European goals
Michael Owen (22)

Highest scoring substitute
David Fairclough (18)

Most hat-tricks
Gordon Hodgson (17)

Most hat-tricks in a season
Roger Hunt (5 in 1961-62)

Most penalties scored
Jan Molby (42)

Most Liverpool games without scoring
Ephraim Longworth (371)

Youngest goalscorer
Michael Owen, 17 years and 144 days v
Wimbledon (A) 6 May 1997

Oldest goalscorer
Billy Liddell, 38 years and 55 days
v Stoke City (h) 5 March 1960

INTERNATIONALS

Most capped player
Ian Rush (67), Wales

Most international goals
Ian Rush (26)

HONOURS

Most player medals
Phil Neal (20)

WINS AND LOSSES

Record victory
11-0 v Stromgodset

Record defeat
1-9 v Birmingham City

**TRANSFER FEES
(as of 2005)**

Record transfer fee paid
£14 million for
Djibril Cisse

Record transfer fee received
£12.5 million for
Robbie Fowler

Riise

VERSATILE NORWEGIAN John Arne Riise was born on 24 September 1980 and started his career with Aalesund. He won the French league with Monaco before joining the Reds' ranks in summer 2001, turning down a counter-offer from Fulham and his former boss Jean Tigana. That same year he was voted his country's 'Athlete of the Year'.

His £4.5 million fee has been amply repaid by performances in both the left back and wide midfield roles, a scorching left-foot shot one of his most potent weapons. 36 caps for his country at age 24 means he should become a centurion in Norway's service, and having been ever-present in his first season at Anfield he remains a key player in Rafael Benitez's plans.

His first goal for his new team was on old team's Monaco's ground, helping win the Super Cup with a 3-2 victory over Bayern. Eight goals in his first season including a spectacular one against old rivals Manchester United in a memorable 3-1 home win made Riise a firm fan favourite, and though he couldn't maintain the strike rate he was given a five-year contract in 2002, underlining his importance to the Liverpool cause.

RIGHT Riise goes for a volley

BELOW Riise in action in 2005

Rush

STRIKER SUPREME IAN Rush was born on 20 October 1961 at St. Asaph, near Rhyl in North Wales. He began his career with local side Chester City, a club he would later return to manage after he hung up his boots, but was soon spotted by Bob Paisley on his way to Liverpool for £300,000 - then a record fee for a teenager.

He made his debut in red against Ipswich in

ABOVE Ian Rush beats goalkeeper Neville Southall of Everton to score their third goal in the FA Cup Final, 1989

December 1980 and, between then and 1987, during Liverpool Football Club's golden era, he was to score a quite remarkable 139 goals in 224 League matches. In many of these games he teamed up with Kenny Dalglish, whose pin-point passes complemented Rush's remarkable pace and accurate finishing; their partnership was rated by many experts the best ever in British football.

One can only imagine the feelings of dedicated Reds fans when Ian Rush decided to leave Anfield in favour of Juventus, following in the footsteps of countryman John Charles. It proved however to be a good move for Liverpool, as they netted £2.75m and, in any case, Rush came back within the year. He just couldn't settle abroad and pined for the scene of his former glories.

His second spell at the club, which lasted until 1996, saw him score slightly less prolifically, but he still managed a further 90 strikes in 245 League encounters. During his career, Rush also

ABOVE Rush in the Anfield changing room for the very last time, reflecting on what will be his last appearance for the club in the FA Cup, 1996

RIGHT Ian Rush takes a shot at goal

in Australia were further stops before retirement.

Ian scored an impressive 346 goals in 658 senior outings for Liverpool, although his total of League goals fell a scant 17 short of Roger Hunt's club record 245. Rush's 49 League Cup goals equals Geoff Hurst. He scored 10 times in 18 Wembley outings with Liverpool, won the League Cup five times, collected five Championship medals and one European Cup and was awarded the MBE.

scored 44 goals in the FA Cup, 39 for Liverpool, which constitutes a 20th century record. His five-goal haul in FA Cup Finals (two apiece in 1986 and 1989 and one in 1992, all for the winning side) is an all-time best.

Rush also continued to score freely for Wales. In all, he made 73 appearances for his country, scoring a record 28 goals and ensuring himself legendary status. He moved to Leeds United in 1996, and to Newcastle a year later, but the goalscoring days were by now largely over. Wrexham (where he was player-coach) and Sydney Olympic

Scott

HAD IT NOT BEEN FOR THE First World War, goalkeeper Elisha Scott (born 24 August 1894) would have played well over 500 games for the club. As it was, his Liverpool career spanned 21 years from his debut on New Year's Day, 1913 – a 0-0 draw at Newcastle – to his final appearance, a 2-0 away defeat to Chelsea, in February 1934. By then he'd clocked up 467 first-team appearances and he remains one of the club's iconic figures. Indeed, to many, Scott is revered as the club's best-ever keeper.

Agile and courageous, Scott played a major role – and missed a mere three League games – as Liverpool claimed the League title in 1921-22 and was ever-present between the sticks the following season as the Championship was retained. He gained the first of 31 caps for Northern Ireland in 1920, the last of

ABOVE Elisha Scott saves a penalty, against Arsenal, 1923

which was earned at the age of 40, two years after leaving Liverpool.

Scott's duels with Everton's centre-forward Dixie Dean were a key feature of the derby matches, with the Reds' keeper constantly reminding the Blues what they had missed out on – he was recommended to Everton before going to Anfield but turned down for being too young. Everton came in for him towards the end of his career but Liverpool fans wrote sacks of protest letters and Scott stayed put until he asked for a move back home to become player-manager of Belfast Celtic.

Shankly

BORN ON 2 SEPTEMBER 1913, THE arrival of Scot Bill Shankly from Huddersfield as manager in December 1959 came after nearly a decade outside the top flight. Rivals Everton prospered until 'Shanks' woke the sleeping giant. He built slowly but methodically, fashioning his side round a central backbone of his countrymen. Goalkeeper Tommy Lawrence, centre-back Ron Yeats and striker Ian St John all hailed from north of the border, and all possessed the qualities of skill, strength and determination Shankly expected of his men. They'd bring top-flight football back to Anfield in 1962, going on to win the League two years later and – finally – the FA Cup in 1965. Their beaten opponents Leeds, managed by the dour Don Revie, would prove to be constant rivals for the coming decade.

RIGHT Shanks salutes the crowd at Wembley after Liverpool had defeated Leeds in the FA Cup Final, 1965

BELOW Bill Shankly pictured in 1969

Shankly had long been used to making headlines – but when he announced Liverpool's record buy, £200,000 Ray Kennedy from Arsenal in July 1974, just months after a second FA Cup win, he used the event to announce he was quitting while he was on top. To the city of Liverpool he was a legend, even if the blue half's respect was grudging, and his death in 1981 – less than a year after another mighty Merseysider John Lennon – would be universally mourned.

SHANKS' WIT AND WISDOM

"Some people believe football is a matter of life and death, I am very disappointed with that attitude. I can assure you it is much, much more important than that."

"Napoleon wanted to conquer the bloody world. I wanted Liverpool to be untouchable."

"No one was asked to do more than anyone else...we were a team. We shared the ball, we shared the game, we shared the worries."

"I was the best manager in Britain because I was never devious or cheated anyone. I'd break my wife's legs if I played against her, but I'd never cheat her."

"I think Dixie would be amazed to know that even in death he could draw a bigger crowd than Everton can on a Saturday afternoon." **Bill Shankly at Dixie Dean's funeral**

"The 'This is Anfield' plaque is there to remind our lads who they're playing for,

and to remind the opposition who they're playing against."

"The problem with you, son, is that all your brains are in your head." **Shankly to a Liverpool trainee**

"If Everton were playing at the bottom of the garden, I'd pull the curtains."

"The fans here are the greatest in the land. They know the game and they know what they want to see. The people on the Kop make you feel great – yet humble."

"Of course I didn't take my wife to see Rochdale as an anniversary present, it was her birthday. Would I have got married in the football season? Anyway, it was Rochdale reserves."

Smith

UNCOMPROMISING IN THE tackle and the toughest defender in the business, it's hard to imagine that Tommy Smith (born 5 April 1945) joined Liverpool from school as an inside forward. Then again, years later, in what was supposed to be his final game for the club – the 1977 European Cup Final – he demonstrated all the hallmarks of a canny striker with a magnificent header that turned the game Liverpool's way.

The 'Anfield Iron' signed for the Reds on his 17th birthday in April 1962 and made his first team bow against Birmingham the following May. During his early days Bill Shankly used to send Smith into action in the number 10 shirt – remember, these were the days when numbers reflected the players' positions; the ploy bamboozled foreign opponents especially who expected him to play much further upfield than he did.

An FA Cup success, Liverpool's first, came in 1965 as Tommy Smith became a fixture in the side, not only surviving a rebuilding phase by 'Shanks' but becoming club captain. Shankly recognised Smith's leadership qualities – suggesting that the rugged defender wasn't born, but quarried! As his eventual total of 637 Liverpool appearances stacked up, so did the winners' medals. He won four First Division titles, two FA Cup, two European Cups (although he missed the 1978 Final after dropping a pickaxe on his foot!), two UEFA Cups and a European Super Cup.

Smith won one England cap, against Wales in 1971, and was awarded an MBE in 1977.

Souness

THE CAREER OF GRAEME SOUNESS has been marked by controversy. Born in Edinburgh on 6 May 1953, the midfielder initially joined Spurs, but was signed by Bob Paisley from Middlesborough for £350,000 in 1978. He had been a hero at Ayresome Park, and for a long time he was a hero at Anfield. Totally committed to the cause, he helped Liverpool win the European Cup three times, the League Championship five times, and the League Cup four times. Between 1978 and 1984 he scored 38 goals in 247 League appearances.

As his playing career then drew to a close, he moved to Rangers as player-manager. Apart from being sent off in his first game, he did well there, but Anfield called him back and he returned as manager in 1991. His attempts to re-vamp an ageing squad were, however, largely doomed to failure, and an FA Cup defeat by Bristol City in 1994 proved to be the final straw.

Since then, Graeme Souness has had a quite remarkable managerial career, if only for the number of clubs with which he has been involved. After Anfield, he moved to the cauldron of Turkey's Galatasaray. Then he returned to England to manage Southampton, before helping Torino return to Italy's top division. After that, it was Benfica and Blackburn, before he went a little further north to Newcastle. Where will it all end?

LEFT Graham Souness, captain of Liverpool, and Di Bartolomei, captain of AS Roma exchange club pennants before the start of the European Cup Final, 1984

BELOW Souness pictured as manager of Liverpool in 1991

Spice Boys

LIVERPOOL'S 'SPICE BOYS' WERE a gang of gifted but erratic players who became better known for their love of a good time than collecting silverware. They played in a Liverpool team that promised more than they delivered, as in the 1996 FA Cup Final against Manchester United. That game will be remembered by fans more for the players' pre-match amble on the pitch in cream Armani suits and designer sunglasses talking into their mobile phones than their performance over 90 minutes. United, businesslike in dark suits, did the business by inflicting a 1-0 defeat.

Three of the so-called 'Spice Boys', goalkeeper David James, winger Steve McManaman and striker Robbie Fowler, all England interna-

tionals, were re-united under Kevin Keegan at Manchester City, leading to 'Old Spice' headlines. As for Liverpool, the replacement of Roy Evans by Gerard Houllier saw the slate wiped clean and the likes of Phil Babb and Jason McAteer headed out of Anfield. Like the singers they were named after, they would never reach the hit parade again.

MIDDLE David James directing his defence in 1999

LEFT Jason McAteer runs with the ball, 1999

Stanley Park

STANLEY PARK, THE SWATHE OF green which separates Anfield and Goodison, is one of Liverpool's largest and grandest open spaces. It's one of a trio of great Victorian parks – Newsham (1868), Stanley (1870) and Sefton (1872) – which opened within five years and is arguably the most architecturally significant. Landscaped by Edward Kemp, who had assisted Paxton at Chatsworth and Birkenhead, it features a grand terrace punctuated by imposing

RIGHT AND BELOW
Stanley Park, on a beautiful summer's day

shelters with expansive bedding schemes once highlighted by fountains. The 45 hectare park opened in 1870 and contains the Gladstone Conservatory (Grade II), built in 1899 by Mackenzie and Moncur who had also constructed the Palm House in Sefton Park.

The whole landscape of Stanley Park will change radically with the construction of the Reds' proposed new stadium, but the phrase 'across the Park' will never be lost from Liverpool folklore.

Staunton

KENNY DALGLISH SIGNED Steve Staunton (born January 1969) from Irish side Dundalk in 1986. The full-back made his Reds debut in a 1-1 draw with Spurs in 1988 and soon after gained the first of 102 international caps for the Republic of Ireland. Impressive performances at left back meant that the young Staunton held his place in a very good Liverpool side, one that reached the 1989 FA Cup Final and gained a 3-2 extra-time victory over

Everton. Arsenal dramatically put paid to hopes of a double, but the League title was theirs the following season.

On the international scene, Staunton was ever-present for the Republic of Ireland as they reached the quarter-finals of the 1990 World Cup. Staunton, though, was sold to Aston Villa by Graeme Souness in 1991 for more than £1m. He enjoyed more success with Villa, winning the a League Cup winners' medal in 1994, and gained further international recognition at USA '94.

As his contract with Villa petered out, Staunton decided to return to Anfield and in a two-year spell he took his appearances total for the Reds to 147 – weighing in with six goals – before moving back to Villa Park.

ABOVE Steve Staunton tackles Kevin Gallacher of Blackburn Rovers

LEFT Staunton at full stretch for Liverpool. He was appointed Republic of Ireland manager in 2006

St John

BORN IN MOTHERWELL ON 7 JUNE 1938, Ian St John began with his home-town club in 1956. The 'Well were happy enough to sell him to Liverpool in 1961, but Bill Shankly had trouble persuading the Board that, at £37,500, St John was a good investment. He did sign him however, and the striker proved to be a very good investment indeed.

An excellent reader of the game, St John had both style and pace. As well as providing dozens of goals for his striking partners, he went on to score 118 times in 426 appearances overall. Although standing only five feet seven and a half inches, he had great aerial ability due to his marvellous sense of timing. During his career, he played 21 times for his native Scotland. It would have been more had Scottish management at that time been less reluctant to include England-based players in the international side.

Playing alongside Roger Hunt and later in midfield, St John became yet another Liverpool legend. While at Anfield, he had his own radio show and

it was clear that he was a natural broadcaster. When he finished playing, he tried his hand at management with Motherwell and Portsmouth, but then began a new career in television. He became particularly famous for the Saint and Greavsie show on ITV.

RIGHT Ian St John pictured in 1968

Supersub

IF EVER A PLAYER DESERVED THE 'supersub' tag it was red-headed striker David Fairclough. Time and again during his debut season of 1975-76, he left the bench to score crucial goals to help the Reds overhaul QPR and claim the First Division title.

Fairclough born on 5 January 1957, made his debut – as a sub – in a 4-0 away win over Spurs in December 1975 and made five starts and nine substitute showings in all that campaign. But it was as the season drew to its climax that he really made his mark, netting seven goals in the final eight games. This run included both goals in the 2-0 victory over Burnley and another brace in the penultimate game of the season, a 3-0 away win over Manchester City.

His most spectacular effort came in the derby encounter with Everton in early April. Only two minutes remained when he seemingly took on the whole Everton team in a mazy run from the halfway line before planting the ball beyond Dai Davies. Fairclough's most famous intervention, however, was scoring the spectacular late winner against St Etienne in the second leg of the European Cup quarter-final in March 1977.

Supersub did, in fact, make more starts (92) than substitute appearances (61) for the Reds, helping them retain the championship in 1976-77 and win the European Cup in 1978 before being transferred to Swiss club Lucerne in 1983. He is now, like so many ex-Anfield favourites, a media pundit.

BELOW Supersub David Fairclough playing for Liverpool in 1977

Thompson

BELOW Thompson holds the League Cup after victory in 1981

BORN ON 21 JANUARY 1954, 17 year-old Liverpudlian, Phil Thompson signed professional forms in 1971 for the club he had supported as a boy. Another of the players to win a host of medals during Liverpool's golden period, the tall young central defender was soon to repay Bill Shankly, and then Bob Paisley, for the faith they showed in him.

Thompson was an Anfield player until 1984, during which time he made 340 League appearances. He also appeared for his country on 42 occasions, playing a pivotal role in the England defence. Strong and intelligent, he soon became a crowd favourite, and was nicknamed 'Pinocchio' due to his larger than average proboscis.

After seeing out his playing days at Sheffield United, his career having been cut short by recurring injuries, Thompson was to return to Anfield in a coaching capacity. He fell out with the management, but later returned as assistant to Gerard Houllier, taking over from him for half a season when he became ill. He spent several months leaping about in the dugout and, at away grounds, cries of "We love Pinocchio" (Italian operatic arias have a lot to answer for) turned to "Sit down, Pinocchio". Phil Thompson now spends Saturdays in the ranks of the Sky TV pundits.

Titles

LIVERPOOL WON THEIR FIRST League title in 1900-01, a last-game win against bottom club West Bromwich putting them ahead of all-conquering Sunderland, followed a season when they themselves had been pipped by Aston Villa.

Further League titles came in 1906, 1922, 1923 and 1947, with just a single season in the then Division Two in 1904-05 spoiling their ever-present record in the English footballing élite. Stars of this period included fearless keeper Elisha Scott, skilful striker Albert Stubbins and flying winger Billy Liddell, who'd serve from 1945 to 1961.

The 1963-64 season saw the Reds' first title under Bill Shankly, repeating the feat in 1965-66 and 1972-73, before Bob Paisley's remarkable run of success. This saw Liverpool bring home the top prize in 1976, 1977, 1979, 1980, 1982 and 1983. Joe Fagan's side achieved the title in 1984, with the final three Championships to date, in 1986 (the League and Cup Double), 1988 and 1990, being won under Kenny Dalglish's player-managership. The total number of title wins is an impressive 18.

The Reds have yet to put their name on the present Premier League trophy, but you can be sure it is top of Rafael Benitez's agenda.

ABOVE Goalmouth action as Liverpool play Chelsea at Stamford Bridge on their way to another title in 1947

LEFT Ronnie Rosenthal, Ian Rush, Ronnie Whelan, Alan Hansen and John Barnes celebrate winning the League in 1990

The Top 10

LEAGUE APPEARANCES

Rank	Player	Years	Apps
1	Ian Callaghan	(1959-1978)	640
2	Billy Liddell	(1945-1961)	495
3	Emlyn Hughes	(1966-1979)	474
4	Ray Clemence	(1968-1981)	470
5	Ian Rush	(1980-1996)	468
6	Tommy Smith	(1962-1978)	467
7	Phil Neal	(1974-1986)	455
8	Bruce Grobbelaar	(1981-1994)	440
9	Alan Hansen	(1977-1990)	436
10	Elisha Scott	(1912-1934)	430

ALL COMPETITIONS

Rank	Player	Years	Apps
1	Ian Callaghan	(1959-1978)	857
2	Emlyn Hughes	(1966-1979)	657
3	Ray Clemence	(1968-1981)	666
4	Ian Rush	(1980-1996)	658
5	Phil Neal	(1974-1986)	635
6	Tommy Smith	(1962-1978	637
7	Alan Hansen	(1977-1990)	623
8	Bruce Grobbelaar	(1981-1994)	579
9	Chris Lawler	(1962-1976)	546
10	Billy Liddell	(1945-1961)	537

ABOVE A triumphant
Liverpool parade their
new silverware to the
jubilant supporters

LEAGUE SCORERS

Rank	Player	Years	Goals
1	Roger Hunt	(1959-1970)	245
2	Gordon Hodgson	(1925-1936)	232
3	Ian Rush	(1980-1996)	228
4	Billy Liddell	(1945-1961)	216
5	Harry Chambers	(1919-1928)	135
6	Robbie Fowler	(1993-2006)	132
7	Jack Parkinson	(1899-1914)	123
8	Sam Raybould	(1899-1907)	119
9	Kenny Dalglish	(1977-1990)	118
10	Dick Forshaw	(1919-1927)	117

OVERALL SCORERS

Rank	Player	Years	Goals
1	Ian Rush	(1980-1996)	346
2	Roger Hunt	(1959-1970)	286
3	Gordon Hodgson	(1925-1936)	241
4	Billy Liddell	(1945-1961)	228
5	Robbie Fowler	(1993-2001)	183
6	Kenny Dalglish	(1977-1990)	172
7	Michael Owen	(1997-2004)	158
8	Harry Chambers	(1919-1928)	151
9	Jack Parkinson	(1899-1907)	130
10	Sam Raybould	(1977-1990)	128

Toshack

JOHN BENJAMIN TOSHACK WAS born in Cardiff on 22 March 1949. He began his career as a forward with Cardiff City (75 goals in 162 League appearances) before moving to Anfield in November 1970. At the time, he was Liverpool's most expensive signing, costing the club £110,000. It was a while before he established himself at his new home, but when he did, he was to form a marvellous double-act with Kevin Keegan.

Toshack was very strong, and he had great aerial power. He scored on 74 occasions during 172 League appearances for Liverpool, before moving to Swansea City as player-manager in 1978. Perhaps influenced by Swansea's long-dead bard, Dylan Thomas, he started to write poetry himself. Rather more importantly however, as manager, he guided his new club from the Fourth to the First Division. Swansea were more or less bankrupted in the process and could not afford to pay top flight wages to the players. Toshack moved on.

Having played for Wales on 40 occasions, John Toshack was later to manage the Welsh side. His managerial skills took him all round Europe and, among other successes, he was to take Real Sociedad to their first Spanish Cup win and Real Madrid to a Spanish League championship.

RIGHT John Toshack playing for Liverpool in 1972

BELOW John Toshack and Kevin Keegan, attacking the Tottenham Hotspur goal, 1977

Traore

BORN ON 1 MARCH 1980, DJIMI Traore's second-half performance in the Champions League Final (which included a goal-line clearance from Shevchenko at 3-3) won over many critics among Reds fans. More suited to centre-back rather than the left-back role he's been asked to play since joining Liverpool in February 1999, he revelled in the 3-5-2 formation that did the business and made it unlikely he would be switching to the blue side of town, as had been rumoured after a much-repeated televised own goal against Burnley inn the FA Cup.

Strangely for a Frenchman signed (from Laval, for £600,000) by Gerrard Houllier, it was only under Benitez that he established himself as first choice; his form allowed John Arne Riise to move into midfield creating an unlikely but effective left-sided combination. He spent the 2001-02 season at Lens and looked likely to be cashed in on until his renaissance. He's been capped at international level for Mali, his chosen country, and in 2006 moved to Charlton, then Portsmouth.

LEFT Djimi Traore tries to fend off Joe Cole of Chelsea during the UEFA Champions League semi-final, 2005

BELOW Djimi Traore pictured playing for Liverpool in 2005

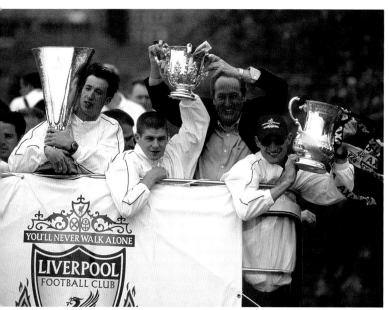

ABOVE Robbie Fowler,
Steven Gerrard,
manager Gerard
Houllier and Sami
Hyypia display
Liverpool's three
trophies, the UEFA Cup,
Worthington Cup and
FA Cup, on a parade
through the streets of
Liverpool, 2001

Trebles

JOE FAGAN, AN ANFIELD BOOT-room regular since 1958, was bidding to emulate Huddersfield and Arsenal, the only teams ever to win three successive Championships. In the event he not only succeeded but went one better than Paisley by adding the Milk and European Cups in a unique Treble. The power on the pitch was provided by combative Scots mid-fielder Graeme Souness, a 350-game veteran who never, ever admitted a cause was lost. The icing on the cake was that Everton had been the Milk Cup Finalists in the first of three all-Merseyside Wembley Finals this decade.

Liverpool's other Treble came in Gerard Houllier's time at Anfield as manager. The Worthington Cup was won in February 2001 – the club's first trophy in six years – to be followed in rapid succession by the FA Cup (against Arsenal), UEFA Cup (against Alaves), Community Shield (against Manchester United) and European Super Cup (Bayern Munich). Such a stunning success rate was impossible to maintain, of course, but having endured the famine Anfield's faithful were happy to gorge themselves at the feast.

UEFA Cup

HAVING REACHED THE EUROPEAN Cup Winners' Cup Final in Glasgow in 1965, only to lose narrowly to Borussia Dortmund of Germany, the Reds and their fans were hungry for more. Yet success in European competition under Bill Shankly eluded them for some time. The first silverware was successfully obtained in 1973 when a two-legged UEFA Cup Final saw them facing German opposition once more in Borussia Moenchengladbach. Inspirational Kevin Keegan scored twice to help his team to a 3-0 home lead, and though Moenchengladbach prevailed in Germany Liverpool hung on to take the trophy with a 3-2 aggregate.

They won the Cup for the second time against Bruges in 1976, again after a hard-fought two-legged tie, squeezing home on a 4-3 aggregate.

Bob Paisley was now in command. The third and so far final UEFA Cup win came in 2001 against Alaves of Portugal under Gerard Houllier. Yet with four Champions League places up for grabs in the Premiership these days, what was once a coveted piece of silverware is now regarded as a consolation prize.

VENISON

Venison

VENISON

RIGHT Barry Venison shields the ball from Mark Robins of Manchester United during the FA Charity Shield, 1990

LIKE HIS LEFT-BACK PREDECESSOR Alan Kennedy, Barry Venison played much of his football in his native north-east for Sunderland and Newcastle. In-between times, the blond bombshell managed to play over 150 games for Liverpool, in the process gaining two League Championships and an FA Cup winners medal as part of the all-conquering team of Kenny Dalglish.

Having written to Liverpool (and all the other top-flight clubs) letting them know of his impending availability, he signed at the end of his Sunderland contract in summer 1986 for £250,000. Barry had already captained his former club to the Milk (League) Cup Final in 1985, the youngest player ever to skipper a side in a Wembley showpiece at 20 years and 220 days.

Six years at Anfield were greatly hampered by injury, and the arrival of

Graeme Souness saw Venison on the move again. Having joined Newcastle in 1992 for another £250,000 fee, he was moved by manager Kevin Keegan from full-back to midfield and as a result won a pair of England caps – at the age of 30 – to add to his Liverpool honours. After brief spells in Turkey with Galatasaray and, later, Southampton, Barry hung up his boots to become a TV pundit.

Whelan

RONNIE WHELAN, ORIGINALLY A rampant Manchester United fan, was born in Dublin on 25 September 1961. Spotted by a Liverpool scout in Ireland, he was signed by the ever-astute Bob Paisley for a very small fee, and he moved to Anfield in 1979. From 1983 onwards, he was a vital member of the side that won almost everything.

Never a prolific goalscorer, Whelan's talent was that of a ball-winner and link man. He operated mainly from the left side of midfield, and often featured in the rapid counter-attacking moves for which Liverpool were famous at the time. He himself scored 73 goals in almost 500 matches, but his tackling ability also sometimes saw him occupying a defensive role. He had tremendous stamina and enthusiasm, was willing to learn and proved extremely adaptable. In other words, he was a true professional.

Whelan played 53 times for the Republic of Ireland between 1981 and 1995, making his debut in April 1981 in a game against Czechoslovakia. Stricken by injury towards the end of his playing career, he moved to Southend United in 1994, later becoming player-manager. He then tried club management in Greece and subsequently became known as an erudite after-dinner speaker.

ABOVE Ronnie Whelan lifts the FA Cup in 1989 after defeating Everton

BELOW LEFT Whelan holds the Charity Shield in 1990 as Barry Venison, Bruce Grobbelaar and Ray Houghton look on

World Club Championship

THE WORLD CLUB CUP, ALSO known as the Intercontinental Cup and the Toyota Cup, is a match played in Japan between the club champions of Europe and South America. It was inaugurated in 1960 by a match between Spanish side Real Madrid and Uruguayan club Peñarol and was created (as the Intercontinental Cup) by Henri Delauney as a way of determining the top club in the world, Europe and South America being the top football continents.

It is not generally considered by European clubs to be a particularly prestigious event, but this may be because South American teams have nearly always won. At all events, as European Champions in 1977, Liverpool elected not to take part. They did however decide that it was worth making the trip in 1981, and again in 1984, but sadly the South Americans prevailed each time.

As everyone knows, the Japanese love football, and each year upwards of 60,000 people have always turned up to see what they hope will be an entertaining game between two of the world's best club sides. They have, however, occasionally been disappointed.

Liverpool fans were certainly disappointed when, at its first attempt, their team lost 3-0 to Flamengo Rio of Brazil in 1981. Three years later the side again found itself in Tokyo, this time going down to a more modest defeat (1-0) at the hands of Independiente of Argentina.

In 2005, the competition was replaced by the Club World Championship, a six-team tournament to feature sides from Africa, Asia, Oceania and Central America. Despite the potential fixture problems their absence would create at home, Liverpool were told they could not withdraw. They slipped to a 1-0 defeat against Sao Paulo in front of a 66,000-plus crowd – a disappointing end to such a brilliant year

Xabi

SPANISH INTERNATIONAL WITH 35 caps at the time of writing who's surely destined for more domestic and international glory. Father Periko starred for Real Sociedad, Barcelona an Spain, but his son looks likely to eclipse his glorious career. A £10 million buy from Real Sociedad in 2004, Alonso (born on 25 November 1981) had steered his club to second in La Liga behind mighty Real Madrid in 2002-03, receiving a national call-up as a reward for his influence. His debut came at age 21 against Ecuador.

He proved his value to the side by his absence after breaking his ankle against Chelsea on New Years Day 2005, but recovered quickly enough to play a part in the run-in to European glory. Alonso missed a pressure penalty in the Final at 2-3 down but recovered quickly enough to net the rebound and set up that nerve-wracking spot-kick shootout (in which he happily didn't have to participate).

"Passing-wise, not many players in Europe are on a level with him," says teammate Jamie Carragher of Xabi Alonso. While his first season saw him play less than 20 games with Steven Gerrard due to Injuries, he excelled in 2005-06, especially in the Reds' FA Cup run.

Yeats

RIGHT Yeats holds up
the 1965-66 League
Championship trophy

BELOW Ron Yeats
enters the pitch, 1969

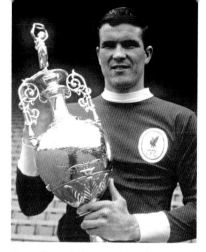

BILL SHANKLY SIGNED RON YEATS (born on 15 November 1947) from Dundee United in July 1961 and at his unveiling suggested the press entourage should "take a walk round him". Big Ron, nicknamed 'The Colossus' by Shanks, would be a giant figure during a 450-game Liverpool career. Before any major successes, however, there was the small matter of gaining promotion from the Second Division: Yeats missed only one league match as Liverpool won the title by eight points.

Two seasons later captain Yeats was lifting the Division One trophy. In fact, for a decade Ron was the rock of Liverpool's defence, making the very most of his physique and ability to read a game. In 1965, he became the first Liverpool captain to lift the FA Cup, after a 2-1 extra time victory over Leeds, while another First Division title came his and Liverpool's way in 1966. Yeats also lead Liverpool in their first forays into Europe, reaching the European Cup semi-finals in 1965, and the Cup Winners Cup Final in 1966, where they were pipped 2-1 in extra time by Borussia Dortmund.

The 1970s saw Bill Shankly looking to rebuild. Yeats played in all but five League matches in 1969-70, but by then Larry Lloyd was being groomed as his replacement. One of Liverpool's greatest defenders and captains, Yeats moved to Tranmere in 1971 and later became their manager. Later still, in 1986, the Colossus returned to Anfield to become the club's chief scout.

You'll Never Walk Alone

AS WELL AS SINGING THE SCOUSE national anthem, 'Ferry Across The Mersey', Gerry and the Pacemakers were responsible for popularising 'You'll Never Walk Alone', from the Rodgers and Hammerstein musical Carousel, as a pop song. The Kop adopted it as their anthem, and history was made.

Gerry and the Pacemakers were the first artists to have Number 1 records with their first three releases, and 'You'll Never Walk Alone' was the third in October 1963. "I'd have made it four with 'I'm The One', says frontman Gerry Marsden now, "but the Searchers (another Liverpool band) stayed on top with 'Needles And Pins'. I kept telling John McNally, John, will you get off the bloody top?"

The mid 1960s was a time when the city of Liverpool simultaneously became the centre of the pop and sporting worlds, Bill Shankly's team giving the crowd something to sing about and many of the songs being supplied by the city's finest groups.

Marsden has noted the song's affinity with football, at Anfield and elsewhere, and in 1988 recorded a new version of 'You'll Never Walk Alone' to raise funds for the Bradford football ground fire appeal. The Kop's own version was sampled on a Pink Floyd record, and John Peel had it played at his funeral. We suspect he's not the only one.

Youth Team

LIVERPOOL'S YOUTH TEAM HAS the good fortune to operate out of one of the finest football academies in the country. Opened in January 1999, the Liverpool FC Academy in Kirkby represents a £10 million investment by the club. The current director is former winger Steve Heighway, assisted by Under-19 coach John Owens and Under-17 coach Dave Shannon.

There are ten grass pitches, four of which are floodlit, and a synthetic pitch made up of rubber granules on a sand base with a two-inch shock absorber underneath that is so realistic it will even take a stud if required. The Academy also boasts a state-of-the-art medical and physiotherapy centre, hydrotherapy pool and weights room, together with offices, seminar and dining facilities for staff and students.

Liverpool have sides ranging in age from Under-9 to Under-17 and Under-19 teams, a total of 180 students being accommodated.

Among the players to have emerged from Liverpool's youth system over the last decade are Michael Owen (a member of the team that won the FA Youth Cup in 1996), Steve McManaman, Robbie Fowler, Jamie Carragher and Steven Gerrard. There are undoubtedly many more to come.

Liverpool retained the FA Youth Cup in 2007 with a dramatic penalty shootout victory over rivals Manchester United.

Zero

KEEPING GOALS OUT was one of the tenets on which Bill Shankly first brought success to Liverpool. It continued under Bob Paisley: Ray Clemence's record of 16 in 42 games in 1978-79 and only four games lost was only beaten in 2004-05 by Chelsea's 15 in 38 games.

But fast forward a decade and the number of clean sheets kept in the 1990s was a cause for concern. Not least in a disastrous 1998-99 campaign, when David James conceded 49 and the club only finished seventh. The arrival of Dutchman Sander Westerveld in summer 1999 showed new manager Gerard Houllier's determination to tighten up at the back, and in his era the goals conceded column was to be admired rather than laughed at. In Westerveld's first season at the club, Liverpool conceded the least amount of goals in the Premiership (30) that year and finished

fourth.

But Houllier moved swiftly after the Dutch keeper blundered against Bolton in August 2001, and a double transfer swoop saw Jerzy Dudek and Chris Kirkland arrive at Anfield on the same day, Westerveld heading for Real Sociedad four months later.

Dudek's 29 clean sheets in his first season helped Liverpool to second place in the Premiership and the UEFA Champions League quarter-finals. A mistake against Manchester United in December 2002 saw Kirkland replace him, but an injury let Dudek back in to excel in the 2003 League Cup final victory against United. Pepe Reina, who arrived in 2005, kept 15 clean sheets in his first 20 Premiership games.

LEFT Sander Westerveld denies Thierry Henry during the FA Cup Final, 2001

BELOW Chris Kirkland gives orders during a match in 2004

Also available:

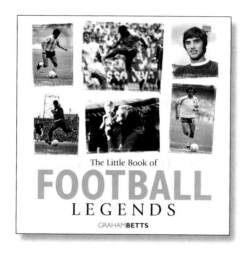

The Little Book of
FOOTBALL
LEGENDS
GRAHAM**BETTS**

Available from all major stockists of books or online at:
www.greenumbrellashop.co.uk

The pictures in this book were provided courtesy of the following:

GETTY IMAGES
101 Bayham Street, London NW1 0AG

PA PHOTOS
www.paphotos.com

Design, artwork and additional photography by Kevin Gardner

Published by Green Umbrella Publishing

Publishers Jules Gammond and Vanessa Gardner

Written by Michael Heatley with David Lloyd and Chris Mason